Stanley Casson

POEMS & PROSE

Compiled by Lucy London / Edited by Paul Breeze

With a Foreword by Lady MacLellan

https://worldofnadjamalacrida.blogspot.com

The Nadja Malacrida Society

This collection published in Great Britain in July 2022 by
The Nadja Malacrida Society which is an imprint of
Posh Up North Publishing, Beckenham Road, Wallasey, United Kingdom

ISBN-13: 978-1-909643-50-5

Publishing History

The poems and tributes on pages 10 to 22 were originally published as "Poems From The Great War by Lieutenant Colonel Stanley Casson (1889-1944) A Solder in the Two World Wars with a foreword by Brigadier SP Robertson" by Napier University, Edinburgh in 2001

"A Brief Biography Of Lieutenant-Colonel Stanley Casson" was originally produced as exhibition panel for Lucy London's WW1 poetry exhibitions held at the Wilfred Owen Story in Birkenhead between 2012 and 2019

"Stanley Casson & Rupert Brook" by Lucy London was originally titled "Rupert Brooke & Skyros" in the "Gallipoli" anthology compiled by Lucy London and published by Posh Up North Publishing in 2015

"Rupert Brooke And Skyros" by Stanley Casson with woodcut illustrations by Phyllis Gardner was originally published in 1921 by Elkin Mathews, London

"A Lost Hero Of The Authors' Club" by CJ Schüler was originally posted on the website www.cjschuler.com in May 2018

"Mystery Flight" was originally posted on the website of the Wartime Heritage Association

LIST OF CONTENTS

Front Cover Photo: Captain S Casson, 3rd Battalion East Lancashire Regiment (Photo by Lafayette Ltd, August 1918 / (IWM)

Back Cover Photo: Portrait photo of Stanley Casson, taken at the outbreak of World War 2

Jennifer MacLellan in her beloved garden in Scotland

FOREWORD

By Lady MacLellan

I am Stanley Casson's daughter.

I was born in 8 New College Lane in 1931 and lived there till my father was called up just before WW2 started, as he was in the Reserve

He returned to Oxford after WW1 and found he was the one in ten who had survived, so felt too depressed to start teaching and found a job as assistant Director at the British School of Archaeology in Athens where he recovered from the trauma of the war.

It was there that he was asked to arrange for the marble tombstone to be laid on Rupert Brooke's grave in the olive grove, by Mrs Brooke, his mother.

As he said, he had not known him but RB was of his generation and it seemed the right thing to do.

As you know my father wrote several books, on quite a few subjects from the technical one on Macedonia, to pre history, philosophy, modern sculpture, both wars, etc. Also many, many articles to various journals of the day.

Thank you for writing about him. How amazed he would be at the developments of IT in our world and all the progress that has followed on from his interviews in the thirties of prominent artists on BBC Radio. (Another book).

With all best wishes

Lady MacLellan (Jennifer)

Lucy giving a talk at the Wilfred Owen Story in Birkenhead in March 2018
(Photo by Paul Breeze)

Stanley Casson - How it came about

In March 2012 Paul and I went to see a production of the musical drama "Bullets and Daffodils" by Merseyside singer/songwriter Dean Johnson. The play is about the life and work of Wilfred Owen, who was brought up and educated on the Wirral Peninsula.

The performance took place in the North Euston Hotel in Fleetwood, Lancashire, which was taken over by the Army in WW1 as the Headquarters of their Gunnery School, whose firing ranges were on the nearby golf links. Wilfred was based there in November 1916 while in command of a 5th Manchester Regiment Battalion.

I was very impressed by the play and by the troupe who performed it and stopped to chat with them afterwards. I found out then about the Museum dedicated to the memory of Wilfred Owen – the Wilfred Owen Story (WOS) – on the Wirral Peninsula, run by Dean Johnson and a group of dedicated volunteers.

I offered to help out behind the scenes. Owing to ongoing health issues I could only write letters/research, etc. and I tried to find more venues in which "Bullets and Daffodils" could be performed.

The play was taken to Craiglockhart in Edinburgh, Scotland, which in WW1 was a Hospital for those suffering from Shell Shock and where Wilfred Owen and Siegfried Sassoon first met. It is now part of the campus of Edinburgh University. While there, Dean noticed a slim volume of poems with the title "Stanley Casson .....".

Knowing of my interest in WW1 poets, he purchased a copy and gave it to me. Dean also asked us to produce an exhibition about female poets of WW1 for display in the WOS in November 2012.

I enjoyed reading Stanley Casson's poems and contacted his daughter Lady MacLellan to ask her permission to mention him on one of our Forgotten Poets of WW1 exhibition panels. So began a wonderful pen friendship. In April 2015, Jennifer kindly agreed to become the Honorary President of our Commemorative Exhibition Project (see www.femalewarpoets.blogspot.com).

Jennifer told me about her father's book "Steady Drummer", which was originally published in 1935, and I was given a re-printed copy for Christmas 2020.

I read it and loved it but I felt it was a shame that there was no biography of Stanley Casson nor mention of his poems in the reprint.

After all, Casson had a very interesting life as a volunteer soldier in WW1 and an archaeologist and he also wrote many other books.

Therefore, in order to fill that gap, Paul suggested we produce this volume ...

Lucy London

THE POEMS

In the original 2001 edition of Stanley Casson's poems, his daughter Jennifer MacLellan wrote:

"Not long ago, I discovered a small notebook in my father's papers which contained poems which he had written during the First World War."

She adds here:

"The little notebook is the only evidence that he wrote any poetry.   Everything else is prose."

"I imagine, in the long pauses between action, in the trenches, he filled in the waiting time, by writing some poems. It would have occupied his mind and his sister's notebook and a pencil, would have been the only tools available."

Sapt Eroi Ungaii
(Epitaph near the Predeal Pass in the Carpathians)

Seven Magyars' bones are laid
Within this sheltered fir-crowned shade.
Poor disembodied spirits they
Fast-held in the Transsylvan clay.
Pity them not; had they been free
The soil on them would cover me.

Micklegarth

Who thunders at the Golden Gate?
Whose is the banner wide unfurled?
Into whose waiting basket falls
The Crimson Apple of the World?

Antrosophy

What coloured cubes, what beds of clay
What crystal clusters you will find
Along that narrow path within
The spangled caverns of the mind

Gallipoli

Where once Achilles stood I stand,
The same waves foaming over the same sand.
His thoughts are mine, my courage his.
Ours are the self-same histories.

But me no Nereid stands beside.
Life is my guardian, Death my guide.
The far peaks gleam, my course is set.
Ours the same race and the same debt.

Ploughboy Soldiers

These men were young and all they owned was
youth;
They knew the rising and the set of day;
They knew the clouds and fields; their store of
Truth
Was blended with the cornfields and the clay.

This was their landed property, for they were born
From rich inheritance of years untold;
They gave it all to make new fields of corn
To grow new valleys rich with August gold.

Lieut-General (Ypres)

As you sat in the evening, reading,
and warm by the fire
(The snow-flakes vainly, push at the window,
aimlessly striving)
Do you remember those sad five thousand spirits
You launched one day, so many years ago now?
Off they flew in the night, sadly and softly crying
Flashed as they passed,
like sparks from a hard-braked wheel,
Off to the coldness of space, unseen forever.

You'll hand launched them those years ago,
can you remember?
Still they aimlessly tap at your window,
softly like fingers
Of cold snow, wanting to tell you
and make you recall them.

To My Skull

Here in this battered box I sit
Side by side withWoe and Wit
How shall longer time be spent
In so bizarre a tenement?

Dextera Dei

Unnumbered are the wonders of the mind of man
Uncounted his inimitable achievements,
Manifestations of his unconquered mind,
Thoughts made concrete, set and solid.
All these, they tell us, are but faint images
Of the immortal mind,
whose great and concrete invention
Is the slow-revolving,
evolving and decaying, universe.
Yet when the ants of man are hopelessly,
and irretrievably ruined byActs of God
It seems that something has gone wrong
and there is some lack of harmony
Somewhere. Somehow it just doesn't seem to
work.

Ploegsteerdt Wood

He never saw the Waggon roll
Its nightly circle round the Pole;
Nor watched the fumes of dawn's dim light
Drive off the terrors of the night,
Nor heard its vernal ecstasies
As Death went singing through the trees.
Untried, untouched, he only fears
The echoes of those flaming years.

Soldier's Prayer

O Lord, of us who fight this battle
Some will be maimed or killed like cattle.
O Lord, of all thy loving kindness
Save me from death or wounds or blindness.
O Lord, if thou shoulds't think of it,
Let anyone but me be hit.

The Royal Road

Alexander (who shall say?)
Drifts across this dusty way.
And the soil that once was king
Hides the sun's pale glimmering
Kings may die yet he shall reign
In his golden dust again.

The Wild Bird (after the Greek)

Now your slender voice is still
That echoed over moor and hill;
How silently you take your flight
Through the dim pathways of the night.

Achilles In Hell

Who strides in joy nor heeds the breath
Of Asphodel, flower-scent of death?
What clash of bronze is this that calls
Old echoes from these twilight halls?
Achilles passes; a bright gleam
Lightens and fades as fades a dream.

Tomb

Stranger, pause a little span:
This is my tomb; my name is Man.
With brittle stone but lasting skill
I bent the forest to my will.
The wild l caught or killed or tamed;
I thought, and all my thoughts I named.
Song, grief and laughter - these I bred
In a mad world imprisoned.
Suckled by earth, earth-free I give
My immortality to you - you live.

Aristeas In Caucasus

Here is the end of men's desires –
These curious domes, these gilded spires!
The full sail sags, the anchor falls
Splashing these strange and blood-red walls.
Here two and seventy peoples dwell
Each in a fabled citadel.
The two and seventy tongues they speak
Are nowhere heard where men hear Greek

Let your ship not, its cargo drown;
Forget the old world, clamber down
These glistening road ways: (through the gate
The sunrise strikes immaculate).

Up to the frosty ridges; then away
and down to where live men
Who know not love nor grief nor death
Nor anything which perisheth.

Here take your rest, here point your tent
At a more starry firmament.

Omission

When the earth is a ball of ice and the stars have
fallen
And interstellar space is darker than ocean deeps
And all mind and thought had fled back to its
source and centre
Whence it once so uselessly idly proceeded:
One lone thought, my own, blind lost and forgotten
Flutters endlessly through the frozen dark, round
and round forever
I made it; no-one ever fashioned the like before; it
wavers
And leaves still something not given on loan, one
useless feather
Of mind, man-made, my own, defying the rolling
wheels of creation.

Dead Lover

A thousand years ago I died,
Nor saw your face; but now my dust
Stirs at your feet and all that wide
Unending stretch of time is thrust
To vacuous space; I feel your tread
And see your lips - and Time is dead.

Helen's Mirror

This is the mirror she gazed in; this held her face;
Here in the serious unreal depths
her eyes looked for a space
At their own dark shadows,
and gazing she thought and pondered
And saw that lovely turn of her neck
and the dark curls, and wondered
Idly, letting her delicate thoughts drift gently.

Now the mirror lies in my hand;
but the shadows have drowned it
Nothing moves in its depths,
and its surface is steel, around it
Lifeless and dead lies a winter's calm
as when ice has bound it.

Commemorative plaque placed by a grateful country on the house of a war-hero (now a miner)

Here lives James Albert Smith, VC
And DCM (with bars);
He earns enough per year to keep
Lord L-nsd-le in cigars.

No Title

Long years ago men sought to find
Secret enchantment of the mind –
Lead turned to gold, some crystal grail,
Some secret armament of mail,
Some hidden name whose myotic power
Brought cities tumbling in an hour;
Some garnet talisman, whose light
Brought blood-red ruin in a night.
They never sought what now I hold;
They searched the stars, they scoured the night
And never found that glistening gold,
That crystal chalice of delight.

O.B.E.

Rule Britannia, o'er the waves
Outpost Britons dig their graves,
And they strive for masters' gain
Pour supprimer l'indigène.
With equal care their masters fit on
Manacles to every Briton.

This is a copy of the poem *Lieut-General (Ypres)*
from Stanley Casson's original notebook

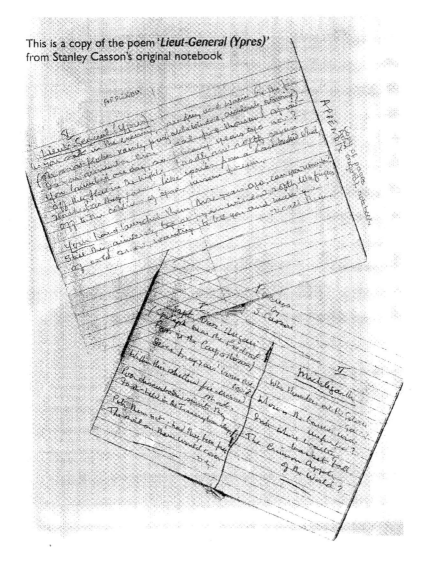

Professor Myres, (Fellow of New College and Professor of Ancient History at Oxford) in his 1944 obituary, wrote:

"Stanley Casson combined in an unusual way the qualities of a scholar and connoisseur with those of a man of action and adventure".

"In the Greek journal Hellas you will find his epitaph'.

'The monuments he loved in peace
He strove to shield in war
And gave his life for them and Greece
Upon a distant shore'

"For behind critical smile and cynical phase, Casson was an optimist. Capable of great happiness, and exceptionally happy in the congenial companionship of his wife and adoring daughter, 'more precious than his own life'. "

On reading the poems in 2001

D. Drever Bed, MPhil, Head of English department, Kirkwall Grammar school, said:

Clearly he brings a scholar's frame of reference to the classical allusions of many of the poems. What places him as a poet of his time are wryly wrought lyrics of survival. There is a sardonic twist to them that is very much in keeping with the survival poetry of WW1: he certainly speaks eloquently for the "puir bloody squaddie'.

The quartet of lines, Number 19, has a bitter twist that puts me in mind of both Siegfried Sassoon's iconoclastic poems and Joe Corrie, the Scottish coalminer poet': anti-establishment sallies.

Helen McPhail, Chairman, Wilfred Owen Association:
"I imagine we will still be hearing of such matters when the centenaries of 1914-18 come round: it's no wonder that we need poets to recall the mood of those times, when events seemed to exceed the capacity of ordinary prose records".

"I am not surprised that Lady MacLellan was pleased to discover them - they must be a wonderful reminder of her father."

"It seemed a great pity that he did not include any of this material in his autobiographical writings, but presumably he preferred to keep his poetry to himself; it is so often the deepest feelings that demand expression in the form of poetry and it is often not easy to share such material with others."

"With few exceptions they have something valid to say, and for the most part they say it with elegance and wit. Helen McPhail rightly points to the classical influence on his subject matter and style. There is a fine epigrammatical bite to some of the pieces, including several of the war poems"

A Brief Biography Of Stanley Casson
(1889 - 1944)
By Lucy London

Portrait photo of Stanley Casson taken at the outbreak of World War 2

Stanley Casson was born in 1889 to William Augustus - a civil servant and barrister - and Kate Elizabeth (née Peake) Casson was educated at Merchant Taylors School in London.

He studied Classics at St. John's College, Oxford, and in 1913 was elected to a Studentship at the British School of Archaeology in Athens.

He became fluent in Greek and undertook pioneering studies of Greek history and art, including the second volume of a new catalogue of the collections of the Acropolis Museum.

On 15th August 1914, Stanley was granted a commission with the 3rd Battalion of the East Lancashire Regiment as a Second Lieutenant and joined his regiment in Flanders. In 1915, he was wounded in action and was promoted to full Lieutenant on 15th May.

On 1st March 1916, Casson was seconded for service on the Staff and this was probably when he joined the General Staff in Salonika under General Sir George Milne, Commander-in-Chief of British Troops.

While on the Staff, he was promoted to temporary Captain, trekked through the desert in Turkestan and was one of the first British officers to enter Constantinople.

For his service he was mentioned-in-despatches and appointed a Chevalier of the Order of the Redeemer, Greece's highest order.

After the First World War, Stanley Casson became Assistant Director of the British School at Athens. He directed British Academy excavations in Constantinople in the late Twenties. During this period he published thirteen books of archaeology, art history, philosophy and autobiography.

While he was in Athens, he was approached by a friend at the British Legation regarding the placing of a tomb over the grave of Rupert Brooke. Rupert Brooke had died of an illness on board ship en route for Gallipoli in 1915 and, under orders to depart for Gallipoli, his friends in the Division had buried him hastily in a secluded dell - Olive grove - three hundred feet above sea level, surrounded by olive trees and bordered with the lovely flowers that bloom in Greece in springtime.

Brooke's mother was determined that Rupert should have a proper grave and, with his knowledge of Greek sculpture, Casson was the ideal person to supervise and organise the construction and transport of the two and a half tons of marble that you will see if you visit Brooke's grave today.

The logistics of the operation are quite remarkable and are detailed in a book called "Steady Drummer" written by Stanley Casson and published in 1935 by G. Bell of London.

In February 1924, Casson became engaged to Nora Elizabeth Joan Ruddle, daughter of the late George Ruddle, owner of the famous Rutland Brewery.

The couple married on 9th August 1924 at All Souls Church, Langham Place, London. It was a quiet ceremony attended by family members only as Casson's father had just died a short time beforehand and Joan's parents had both died within a short time of each other the previous year.

After a honeymoon on the continent, the couple settled in Oxford and they had a daughter Jennifer in 1931.

After his marriage, Casson returned to New College, Oxford, as Reader in Classical Archaeology. He used to give talks on BBC wireless about archaeology and sculpture and interview famous artists of the day and later in the 1930s, he also spent time in America as he had a visiting Professorship to Bowdoin College, Maine.

Casson had already been a Reservist prior to WWII and on 2nd September 1939 he was appointed a Lieutenant on the Special List and assigned to the Intelligence Corps. By December, he had been promoted to temporary Major and appointed Staff Officer 2nd Grade at the Intelligence Training Centre.

Although assigned to the Intelligence Corps, Casson was not formally transferred to the Corps until 17 January 1942. Prior to this, he had seen active service in Holland with the British Expeditionary Force, narrowly avoiding being taken prisoner of war when the Germans invaded.

On 7th November 1940, he was promoted to acting Lieutenant Colonel and Specially Employed as G.S.O. 3rd Grade.

In November 1940, Casson flew via Gibraltar and Cairo to Athens to set up a British military mission, with the objective of reinforcing the Greeks in their fight against the Italians.

When Germany invaded Greece, the Military Mission had to withdraw hurriedly, back to Cairo, in order to save men and materials for the North Africa campaign. They were rescued by the Royal Navy, taken to Crete and thence to Cairo, ahead of the German invasion of the island.

On his eventual return to London, Casson worked in the Baker Street office handling the soldiers who were organising resistance by the Greeks to the German occupation. Several of his pre-war students at Oxford were leading the operation, living in the mountains, disrupting railway lines and roads.

In every theatre of war during his career, he was always involved in Military Intelligence, gathering information about enemy movements from prisoners and any other sources. His knowledge of Greek and several other languages was an obvious asset to this work.

Casson was officially employed by the SOE (Special Operations Executive) for his trip to Greece in April 1944 to mediate with the Greek Monarchists and Communists in an attempt to avoid the civil war which, sadly, followed the liberation.

Unfortunately, we will never know what his intervention in that situation might have achieved as the aircraft of RAF Transport Command in which he was travelling crashed into the sea on 17th April 1944, killing all on board.

Casson is buried at Fairpark Cemetery in Newquay, Cornwall.

Rupert Brooke (1887 - 1915)

Stanley Casson & Rupert Brook
by Lucy London

Rupert Brooke was already a well known and published poet before the First World War. He was commissioned into the Royal Naval Volunteer Reserve as a Sub-Lieutenant, joining the Hood Battalion, 2nd Brigade, R.N. Division and took part in the Royal Naval Division's expedition to Antwerp in Belgium.

Rupert's Division set sail from Avonmouth near Bristol for Gallipoli in the Union-Castle Line ship "Grantully Castle" which had been converted for use as a troopship. Among the ships escorting the flotilla of over 200 ships heading for Gallipoli was the Dreadnought Battleship "The Prince George".

The ships put into Cairo in Egypt, where Rupert became seriously ill with a fever and dysentery. An initial landing at Gallipoli was postponed and the ships were diverted to islands in the Aegean Sea.

When the "Grantully Castle" arrived in the Aegean, the anchorage at Lemnos was already already full of ships, so Rupert's ship put into Trebouki Bay off the Island of Skyros.

Skyros is to the east of the mainland of Greece and is one of the Sporades Archipelago in the Aegean Sea (sporades being Greek for "those scattered"). Rupert and the other members of the Hood Battalion went ashore on Skyros for manoeuvres.

They were resting in a small olive grove about 300 metres above sea level, when Rupert was stung on the face by a mosquito and his health, already impaired, deteriorated rapidly.

According to her log, the French Naval Hospital Ship " 'Duguay-Trouin' was at anchor in the bay at Trebouki Bay, having taken on coal in Alexandria", when Rupert Brooke was transferred to her by cutter from the "Grantully Castle".

Rupert was described as "...a Lieutenant on General Hamilton's staff". The Log continues "Wireless messages come in. General Hamilton and Winston Churchill are worrying."

In spite of the efforts of "the whole medical staff mobilised for the single patient" (as there were no wounded for them to treat at that stage) Rupert died on 23rd April. When his death was announced: "Everybody is silent. Then a voice says: "England has lost her greatest poet"."

Arrangements had to be made speedily for Rupert's burial as orders had come through to proceed to the Dardanelles. Rupert had commented upon the tranquility and beauty of the Olive Grove in which the troops had rested during manoeuvres so it seemed the ideal place to bury him.

The log of the "Duguay-Trouin" described the funeral as follows: "The coffin is placed on the poop and covered with the English flag. Sixteen palms decorate improvised chapel.

The officers of the "Duguay-Trouin" lay on the coffin a bunch of wild flowers stolen from the bees of the Island and with the French colours" (red, white and blue) "At the foot of the coffin stands a sailor presenting arms.

Lieutenant Arthur Asquith (1883 – 1939) – one of the sons of Herbert Henry Asquith, the British Prime Minister in the early days of WW1 – who "has not left his friend for a moment, is at the side of the bier with some other English officers. A brief twilight. Then night falls."

Rupert Brooke's original grave on Skyros

As there was "no time to engrave a brass plate, the Lieutenant calls for a soldering iron. Then, by the light of the lamps which are like a wreath of watch lights, he scars on the oak plank itself these letters: *RUPERT BROOKE*

A sharp whistle is heard. The ship's company lines up with bared heads to pay the last honours. A launch takes the boat which carried the coffin in tow. Other boats pull off from the (other British) warships ("Campus" "Prince George" and "Prince Edward"). There are many of them."

"Some olive trees in a more fertile hollow. At their foot a grave has been dug."

William Denis Browne, the composer, critic and pianist (who was known as Denis) was one of Rupert's friends and was also at Rupert's side when he died. Denis, commissioned into the Royal Naval Division at the same time as Rupert, was killed in Gallipoli on 4th June 1915.

Another friend present was Forgotten Poet Patrick Shaw-Stewart, who played an important role in Rupert's funeral being in charge of the firing party and was himself killed on the Western Front in December 1917.

Other members of the Hood Battalion group "Latin Club", as the Rupert Brooke circle was called, who were present at Rupert's funeral, were

- Charles Lister (son of Lord Ribblesdale), who died after being wounded at Gallipoli in August 1915,

- Bernard Freyberg, VC (1889 - 1963) who transferred to the British Army - Queen's (Royal West Surrey) Regiment - in May 1916, and

- Frederick Septimus Kelly*, Australian/British musician/composer, who was wounded twice at Gallipoli and killed on the Western Front in November 1916.

After the First World War, Stanley Casson was working as Deputy Director at the British School of Archaeology in Athens when he was approached by a friend at the British Legation regarding the placing of a tomb over the grave of Rupert Brooke.

Rupert's mother had commissioned a sculpted marble grave in memory of her son. Casson was the ideal person, with his knowledge of Greek sculpture, to organise and supervise the transport and construction of the two and a half tons of marble that you will see if you visit Brooke's grave today.

The logistics of the operation were quite remarkable and are detailed in a book called "Rupert Brooke And Skyros" written by Stanley Casson and published in 1921 and also in Casson's wartime memoir "Steady Drummer" (1935)

Lady MacLellan has kindly sent me a copy of the section concerning the grave of Rupert Brooke. Casson had to hire a boat to transport the marble, then get to the island himself.

Once there, he had to build a small jetty for the unloading of the seven or so crates containing the marble. Once on land, there was the problem of getting the crates up the hill to the site of the grave via the only road which, at that time was a rough goat track.

Nothing daunted, Casson cut wooden rollers from pine trees and began to level the track by removing outcrops of rock on the path. That alone took over a week. Then the crates had to be pushed up the track and Casson mentioned how much he admired and respected the architects of Stonehenge.

During the evenings, Casson spent time with his hosts the local shepherds and goatherds on the island who offered him hospitality and shelter in their shack. After a supper of bread and milk, they would sit round an open fire, talking about the war with the shepherds, some of whom had served in a Greek Division sent to Odessa with other Allied troops.

Returning briefly to Athens to fetch some tools to complete the task, Casson enlisted the help of the author Norman Douglas who had just arrived there. The pair returned to Skyros and oversaw the completion of the laying of the marble tomb over Brooke's grave. Finally, Casson had the tomb consecrated by the head of the local monastery of St. George.

Brooke's replacement grave on Skyros (Photo by Commonwelath War Graves Commission)

Casson reflected: "I wondered what Brooke would have thought to see this strange assembly. I came away sadly to think that here was still another of my generation accounted for. It was a lonely world now for men of my age."

Casson arranged to have the original wooden crosses that had marked Rupert's grave on Skyros sent back to the Brooke family in Rugby, where they were put on the family burial plot. By 2008 the crosses had weathered and were replaced. The originals are now at Rugby School.

"Akhili Bay From The North" woodcut by Phyllis Gardner

RUPERT BROOKE AND SKYROS
BY
STANLEY CASSON
WITH WOODCUT ILLUSTRATIONS BY PHYLLIS GARDNER

Originally published in 1921 by Elkin Mathews, London

I have to thank the editor of The London Mercury for permission to reprint this essay, which first appeared in that journal in October, 1920. A few minor additions and alterations have been made.

The woodcut Illustrations are done from Photographs which I took in Skyros in April 1920.

"The Grave óf Rupert Brooke" woodcut by Phyllis Gardner

Left to right: "Another View of the Grave", "Akhili Bay From Old Skyros Town", "Entrance to Monastery and Citadel" - woodcuts by Phyllis Gardner

Old Skyros Town from the South (woodcut by Phyllis Gardner)

RUPERT BROOKE AND SKYROS

In the northern part of the Aegean Sea, almost mid-way between the islands of Eubœa and Chios, lie the twin peaks of Skyros. The storms of history have broken round and near the island, but only spent waves have reached its shores.

A few legends, a few of the minor events of Mediterranean history and the records of a few travellers are all that it has to show. And now England, who has never yet figured in its history, must claim a place in its soil and tradition, for in Skyros is the grave and memorial of Rupert Brooke.

A wild and lawless island, inhabited even down to the days when Athens was at the height of its power by half-barbarous peoples, Skyros early became the home of the heroes of legend.

Achilles spent his boyhood on its sands and cliffs before Troy called him:

> *He scoured the lonely cliffs and valleys wild,*
> *Hearing the seagulls call to one another,*
> *While far below the great Aegean smiled*
> *(There dwelt the lady of the seas, his mother,*
> *In the old tale). He thought he could descry*
> *Far off amid the clouds those mountains high*
> *The cradle of his race : far other*
> *The isle of Skyros where he lay beneath the sky.**

> ** From AchUlea, by the late R. M. Heath. 1811.*

Theseus was killed by the king of the island when he fled there from Athens, and centuries later his mighty bones, revered as were the bones of Becket, were carried by the Athenian general Cimon to the Athens that had disowned him.

Of these two the name of Achilles still survives in the name of Akhili, which is given to a landlocked bay on the eastern shore, far the loveliest place in the island, whence on the clearest of summer days one can just discern the distant shores of the Troad.

A memorial of Theseus is perhaps found in a small temple site near the old castle high up on the cliffs. It was a small sanctuary, dedicated in all probability to Theseus as a hero, and it was right on the edge of the sea, almost hanging over the water on an escarpment of the main ridge of rock on which the town is built.

Other traces of old Hellenism linger on the island. The spring of Niphi, on the western side, preserves the name of the Nymphs, the hill-top Areion that of Ares, and Artemi that of Artemis. None of these names is a revival, as is so often the case in modern Greece.

The fact that all the places bearing these names are far out in the wilder parts of the island, and so removed from the archaistic zeal of the village schoolmasters and antiquaries, makes it all the more probable that the names come down to us in true and authentic descent from antiquity.

Niphi is a spring that breaks abruptly from the cliff-side and falls into the sea through a luxuriant grove of fig-trees amongst which cluster a few houses, all in ruins but one. Areion is a bleak summit that rises at the southern end of the island above a valley of olive trees. Shepherds told me that there were " old ruins " on it, but I was not able to get there.

Artemi is just such another peak, rugged and without even the wild thyme and shrubs that one finds elsewhere. In few places on the mainland can one find so many traces of antiquity as here, for Turk, Venetian, and Slav have swept away most of the old place-names in the Peloponnese and in the central provinces.

In antiquity the island was famed mostly for its marble and its flocks. Today it produces nothing else but these that the outside world requires. The marble is coloured, veined with rose and yellow, and there is hardly a Roman palace or an Italian church without it.

From the milk of its goats and sheep are made the finest cheeses in the Mediterranean, hardly known outside Greece. Other industries it has none.

Little changes on the island, and it was famed in Roman times for just those same things that bring it its fame of to-day.

Earlier still its flocks were much in repute, and the only coins which are attributed to the island bear a heraldic device of two goats. The old stock must have vanished long ago, but the same herbs, the same shrubs and the same custom of watering the flocks on sea- water as well as fresh produces as fine sheep and goats to-day as two thousand years ago.

The island is divided almost into two parts by a narrow strip of marshy land, to the north and south of which rise the twin peaks. On each are marble quarries; the northern alone is wooded, and contains the only marble quarries that are still worked.

Pefko Bay the "bay of pines" is the harbour whence the vast blocks of rose-pink marble are shipped, conveyed by curious engines and with titanic effort down a winding track from the quarries, a full thousand feet above. Near the quarries is the wind-swept house of the quarry-master, open to all the winds of the Aegean. From its windows one sees the whole panorama of Eubcea, and northwards the other islands of the northern Sporades and perhaps on clear days Olympus itself indeed a Homeric dwelling-place on Homer's " towering crag of Skyros."

The one village of the island is on the eastern side, near no harbour ; the reason for it being thus placed on the most inhospitable shore, at first not obvious, is plain to those who know what the terrors of piracy meant, right down to the early nineteenth century, to villagers on the islands.

To dwell on a harbour was to invite raids from the pirates or other enemies who sheltered there. From prehistoric times onwards the founders of island towns knew this danger.

Phylakopi the Minoan and Plaka the Hellenic cities of Melos were both remote from the magnificent harbour of the island. The chief city of Lemnos is on its stormiest shore.

Kyme, the oldest city in Eubcea, is on the eastern coast, notorious for its tempests, and unapproachable even to-day to modern vessels except in the summer or in the calmest weather of spring and winter; the safer channel of the Euripos is always chosen by coasting steamers in uncertain weather.

So it is that the two great harbours of Skyros, Kalamitsa Bay and Tris Boukes Bay, remain desert harbours except for a few houses at the head of the one and some shepherds' huts at the other. It is in a valley off Tris Boukes Bay that the tomb of Rupert Brooke lies a lonely valley in a lonely bay, with none but shepherds and storm-bound sailors to see it.

But the war that created a new piracy found new defences against it, and the irony of time brought it about that the very harbours that of old had been the refuge of pirates now became a refuge against them ; while they were kept to the doubtful comforts of the depths of the sea outside, mighty fleets of transports waited their time in these landlocked bays.

So it came about that Rupert Brooke found himself in this desert bay, from which it was not his destiny to depart.

As its name denotes, Tris Boukes Bay is the bay of "Three Mouths." Two small islands lie athwart the entrance, thus forming the three narrow entries.

Despoti, the larger of the two, is so called in island legend because it was once the home, and a barren one at that, of a bishop hermit. Plati, the smaller, is a mere rock. The bay itself is fifteen miles from the one village of the island, and the shore has no fresh water, the nearest spring being Niphi, seven miles away.

To this bay early in April of this year, almost five years after his death, it was my privilege to bring the monument that is now placed over Rupert Brooke's grave.

After one vain attempt to reach the island in March, when a storm off Sunium drove us back to the mainland, I finally reached the island at the dawn of a windy day in the first week in April.

The rugged outline of the island rose against a grey lashing sea with a red and forbidding sunrise behind it. Away to the west was the sharp peak of Mount Delph in Eubcea, curiously like the Japanese prints of Fujiyama, snow-covered and abrupt.

Southwards were the vague outlines of Andros and Tenos. A five hours' walk from the landing-place brought me to the valley in which, two thousand yards from the shore, lay the grave. The wooden crosses still stood undisturbed and intact. The stones over the grave were as when first they were placed there.

The work necessary for the landing of the marble slabs comprising the monument, and for their erection, took the best part of three weeks, for the villagers and masons who carried out the work had to hew a path over the ground to the olive-wood where the grave lies.

Since there were no houses and no village nearer than fifteen miles, we found quarters with the shepherds of the valley and lodged in their huts.

Simple, sturdy folk such as these shepherds come as a pleasing relief after the banalities of the town-living Greek. There was something almost Homeric about their simplicity. The mandra, or shepherd's camp, where I lodged, was the property of one family, its occupants an old patriarch of over eighty (he was not quite certain how much over eighty !) and his six nephews, varying in age from twenty to thirty.

The dwelling-house at the mandra was built high up above the sea on the side of a rocky peak, a shanty made of rocks and strong olive-poles. Inside was a row of shelves, one above the other, that served as beds, a wide open fireplace, and a few low stools.

Every evening at sundown the younger men would drive the sheep and goats back from their pastures to the pen and milk them, while the old uncle busied himself with lighting the fire and preparing the evening meal.

Their work done, all the shepherds would come inside, the door would be closed, for it was cold at nights, and we would eat a meal of bread and milk, cream cheese, and junket in front of the blazing fire.

They were not meat-eating men, nor did they take wine or tobacco except on their rare visits to the village. Their active season of work had begun, and they would stay in the mandra all the spring, migrating later, after the lambs and kids had been weaned, to the hill-tops with their flocks, and sleeping out at nights in the summer on the open hill-sides covered with their heavy woollen cloaks.

In the hut after nightfall we all sat round the fire discussing subjects that ranged from European politics to the price of cheese. Most of the younger men had seen service in the war one in Russia with the Greek forces at Odessa, others in Macedonia or Asia Minor.

One, I found, had been in the same region as myself in the Struma Valley. Yet the war had not spoiled them, and they were once again island peasants wearing the island costume, and eating with wooden spoons from wooden basins.

The Greek countryman has too much of the unchangeable Oriental in his nature to let new-fangled notions take deep root.

Long before dawn the younger men were up and about, leading their flocks to the pastures.

One night returning to the mandra I lost my way and wandered aimlessly and rather hopelessly on the mountain-side.

For once shepherds' dogs proved a blessing, for, hearing me stumbling on the hill-side a mile away, they started barking, and so guided me to the home that I could not see and had thought to be in a very different direction.

As I approached they ran out barking at me, and were only driven off by the showers of stones that their masters hurled at them to enforce obedience. I remembered the passage in the Odyssey where Odysseus, in just such another plight, approached the mandra of Eumaeus and was saved from attack by a similar expedient on the part of the shepherds.

Many curious customs and stories persist among men such as these shepherds.

Their ways of managing their flocks is a study in itself. They control and lead the sheep and goats not with the aid of their dogs, but by a system of cries and shouts which, I was assured, the animals understand, and I was given demonstration of this by one of the shepherds.

There is one series of cries for sheep and another for goats, while for horses, mules and dogs there are quite other, sounds. The shepherds' dogs are used for guarding the flocks from attack of man or beast, or for retrieving lost lambs and kids, and there their duties end. They differ greatly in type from the shaggy brutes of the mainland, and are lithe and swift, not unlike Welsh collies.

The sheep and goats of Skyros are kept together in the same flocks, although there are separate cries used by the shepherds for each. The shepherd can thus, if he wish, separate his animals.

Cheeses are made from the milk of both animals mixed. One shepherd assured me that a great quantity of milk is lost owing to the snakes which come at night and suck the milk from the udders. This belief is, I think, almost universal in Europe wherever there are snakes in large numbers.

Such are the people in whose remote island valley lies this lonely grave. Some of these shepherds had seen the actual burial, and all knew vaguely the story of Rupert Brooke and who he was. In anything that concerns them Greeks are not slow to learn.

The villagers of the one village of the island are of much the same stamp. Nearly all wear the island costume a close-fitting jacket of white wool reaching to the waist, with a blue waistband and breeches and white woollen gaiters.

In the village to this day there survives a dance, unique among the islands or on the mainland of Greece, known as the "Dance of the Old Man." It is a curious primitive beast dance in which shepherds from the hills cover their faces with the skins of hares or martens. They hang fifty or more sheep-bells round their waists and dance up and down the village until they drop from exhaustion.

The dance takes place every day during the week before Lent, and its origin is wrapped in obscurity. It may perhaps have something to do with the old worship of Dionysus in Thrace, whence the present inhabitants are believed to have come some time in the Middle Ages.

The villagers themselves have no explanation of the dance, but still keep it up vigorously and enjoy it. Although it comes in the week before Lent it has no religious significance. With the honesty of Pagans they admit it to be a purely pagan custom ; they could hardly do otherwise.

Above the village on a pinnacle of rock that stands out like a rampart above the long sandy spit known as "Vampires' Cape" is built the old medieval town on the ruins of its predecessor Hellenic Skyros, the colony of ancient Athens.

Round the ruins of this town run the walls, a double gate defending the entrance. The churches alone remain intact and cared for, and with them the monastery of St George, with its wonder-working eikon. Below the old town lies the modern village, covering a hollow of ground as though poured from a funnel, built in the days when piracy had become less of a menace, and when it was safe to live without walls. The white flat-roofed houses glisten as only island towns can glisten in the Aegean sun.

I wonder how many people will visit this remote island to see the grave. It means long and weary journeying, and will be a real pilgrimage. From the sea, just off Tris Boukes Bay, the monument can just be seen, with its white Pentelic marble showing clear through the olive trees, the only visible sign of man or his works at this end of the island.

But none save coasting steamers and caiques pass close to the island, and few will see the tomb save those who go to see it. It lies in a deserted valley at the deserted end of the island. Greek of old, Imperial Roman, and the rest, have never made their dwelling hereabouts, for there is no water, and it is barren soil.

But by some curious fortune one of the villagers who was with me uncovered an ancient tomb on the shore near where the monument was landed. It was almost on the sea edge, and we could find no trace of other burials. There is no proof as to who it was who was buried here save the fact that it was a Roman, and probably a woman, judging by the glass unguent bottles that were in it with the skeleton.

Perhaps it was the grave of someone drowned in the bay, or who had died when some ship had put in here for refuge, even as the ship that brought Rupert Brooke here.

I am reminded of many of the epitaphs in the Palatine Anthology that commemorate the graves of men drowned at sea and buried hard by on the seashore in the lonely bays of Greece. One epitaph, more than most, seems almost as though it had come from such a grave as this. It is from the tomb of a sailor drowned in harbour:

The sea is the same sea every-
where; why do we idly blame the
island rocks, the swift current of
the Straits or the jagged reefs ? In
vain they have their evil fame;
why else did I escape them but
to be enwhelmed in the haven of Scarphe ?

Pray whoso will for a safe passage
home; that the ocean keeps the
ways of ocean still, I, Aristagoras,
know full well, for I lie buried here.

Save for these two graves, the valley is as deserted as when first volcanic forces lifted the marble heads of the islands from the sea. But it is covered with a profusion of wild flowers such as one rarely finds in Greece. Pale blue anemones, orchids, rock hyacinths, and sombre russet fritillaries star the turf, while everywhere is the scent of wild thyme and mint that grows thick between the bushes of wild olive.

The land belongs to the monastery of St George, and one of the monks of the monastery was sent to carry out the ceremony of consecration of the tomb according to the rites of the Greek Church.

For once St George of Skyros and St George of England have met on common ground.

Phyllis Gardner with some of her Irish Wolfhounds at her home in Maidenhead in 1936 (The Illustrated Sporting & Dramatic News, 17th April 1936)

A Few Words About Phyllis Gardner
By Paul Breeze

Phyllis Gardner (6th October 1890 – 16th February 1939) was a writer, artist, and latterly known as a breeder of Irish Wolfhounds. She attended the well known Slade School Of Fine Art in London and was a suffragette supporter when she met Rupert Brooke.

They became friends and the pair had a sort of "on- off" relationship, however it was all shrouded in mystery for much of the 20th century as Gardner's memoir about her involvement with Brooke - along with their letters to one another - were deposited by her sister Delphis in the British Library in 1948 and closed to access for 50 years.

Lady MacLellan told us how her father came to get Phyllis Gardner to illustrate his Skyros book:

"Phyllis' father - Ernest Arthur Gardner - was a Professor of Greek History and was the Director of the British School of Archaeology in Athens so he may have been there when Stanley Casson was the Assistant Director after WW 1."

"SC wrote a Chapter on Constantinople at the end of Gardner's book 'Greece and the Aegean'. They were clearly good friends."

"With her father being a colleague of my father's, he would have seen Phyllis's work - which was very good - and chosen her to illustrate his book."

"After Phyllis Gardner's letters were removed from their 50 year embargo, Lorna Beckett wrote a book about the secret romance that she'd had with Brooke. Fascinating! It was rather a case of unrequited love, I fear, but Rupert was so fascinating to so many women, that she really had no chance."

"Phyllis had clearly wanted to keep her relationship with RB secret, hence the 50 year embargo."

Phyllis never married and, in later life, her family successfully bred Irish Wolfhounds and opened a kennel called Coolafin in Maidenhead.

Phyllis wrote a well-regarded history of the breed, entitled "The Irish Wolfhound – A Short Historical Sketch" (Dundalk: Dundalgan Press, 1931) which she and her sister illustrated with over 100 woodcut illustrations.

Phyllis and her sister never married and, after their parents' deaths, they remained at the farm in Maidenhead, along with their younger brother Christopher - who had learning difficulties.

Phyllis died of breast cancer at the relatively young age of 48 and was buried close to her parents' grave in the churchyard of St James the Less Church, Stubbings, Maidenhead, Berkshire.

Christopher, Phyllis and Delphis Gardner with Irish Wolfhound puppies (Irish Wolfhound Yearbook, ca. 1932)

Having discovered that her grave was unmarked and been untended for many years, the – sadly, now defunct - Rupert Brooke Society ran a successful appeal to raise funds for a headstone.

After Phyllis's death, Delphis struggled to look after her brother and the property and the dogs suffered from the privations and rationing brought in during war.

In 1947, she was prosecuted and fined for failing to look after the 11 dogs in her care properly and in 1949, Delphis sold the Maidenhead property and took Christopher to live on a farm at Curracloe in Ireland.

They lived there as virtual recluses but were indulged by the locals and had a housekeeper to cater for their basic needs.

Delphis died of pneumonia at Wexford County Hospital in 1959, - and Christopher in 1968 - and they were both buried in Ardcolm Churchyard.

For more about Phyllis and Rupert Brooke, read: "The Second I Saw You: The True Love Story Of Rupert Brooke and Phyllis Gardner" by Lorna C Beckett - Chair of the Rupert Brooke Society (London: The British Library Publishing Division, 2015).

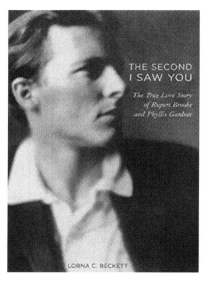

PREFACE to

Catalogue of the Acropolis Museum Volume II – Sculpture and Architectural Fragments

By Stanley Casson, MA

Fellow of New College, Oxford and Assistant Director of the British School at Athens

First published by the Cambridge University Press in 1921

THE delay in the appearance of Volume II of the Acropolis Museum Catalogue is due to the European war. The section dealing with the Sculptures and Architectural Fragments was completed in the summer of 1914 and, together with the section dealing with the Terracottas, which was completed some time previously, was actually sent to the Press by July 27th, 1914.

Not until May, 1919, did events allow me to return to the MSS, when publication became possible, thanks to the kindness of the Cambridge University Press, who renewed their desire to proceed in the matter, and of the Hellenic Society who had again expressed their wish to see the volume produced.

Volume I dealt with all the Sculptures in the Museum of a date preceding the invasion of Xerxes in 480 b.c. The Sculptures herein described belong, with one exception, to periods after that date. The architectural fragments and other antiquities belong to periods both before and after 480 b.c.

The comparatively portable nature of this volume enforces upon it limitations for which I can only apologise by saying that they are unavoidable. Thus the illustrations are for the most part only sufficient for the identification of objects and are not intended to be descriptive plates ; they are included in the text so as to avoid the somewhat tiresome searching for plates which would be necessary were they published separately or at the end of the volume.

It is regretted that it has been impossible, owing to the limitations already pleaded, to provide illustrations of everything described. In the case of the Erechtheium and Parthenon sculptures, however, references are given in each case, where an illustration is lacking, to the best available illustrations in other publications, such as the Antike Denkmaler plates of the Erechtheium fragments and the British Museum plates of the Parthenon fragments.

My thanks are due in the first instance to the Greek authorities who in 1913 and 1914 gave me every facility for work in the Acropolis Museum and its annexes, and to Miss C. A. Hutton and Mr A. H. Smith by whose kindness and help I was able to carry out the preliminary work on the casts of the Acropolis fragments in the British Museum.

I am further indebted to Mr Smith for the use of copies of the plates of the British Museum publication on the Parthenon and for information recently given as to changes and alterations in the arrangement of the frieze. One of the results of the research which the compilation of this catalogue involved has been that some additional casts of fragments have been added to the Parthenon frieze as now set up in the British Museum.

The section on Terracottas is the work of Mrs J. R. Brooke, M.B.E. (Miss Dorothy Lamb), and was written when Mrs Brooke was a student of the British School. I have recently revised the whole of the MSS in the light of publications subsequent to July 1914 and my particular thanks are due to the Cambridge University Press for the safe custody of the MSS from July 28th, 1914, to May 17th, 1919.

During my revision of the MSS and the correction of proofs much help was afforded me by Professor P. Gardner and Professor R. M. Dawkins. To Mr A. M. Woodward I am indebted for much information in regard to the inscriptions, based on notes made by him when in Athens.

I am indebted to Messrs Alinari of Florence and to the British Photographic Company, Athens, for the use of a number of photographs both of the Parthenon frieze and of some of the miscellaneous sculptures.

My record of thanks would be but half expressed were I to omit mention of all the kindness and help of the late Guy Dickins who read through the whole of the MSS in the spring of 1914. In his death Archaeology has suffered an irreparable loss.

S. CASSON.
New College, Oxford.
December, 1920

PREFACE to "XXTH Century Sculptors" by Stanley Casson

First published by Oxford University Press in 1930

Reprinted in 1967 by Books For Libraries Press Inc, Freeport, New York USA.

This book is, in a sense, a sequel to my other entitled Some Modern Sculptors – published in 1928. The growing interest in sculpture which seemed to be indicated by the demand for the first book has encouraged me to deal with some of the more recent developments and with other living scultors whom, for lack of space, I could not discuss in my previous essays.

No doubt some critics will complain that I have omitted many living sculptors. To them I can only reply that this small book is not an exhaustive treatise but a short account of the work of men who seem to me to be the most interesting of modern scuptors.

There are still many young artists who have yet to form their style and establish their reputation and among them I think I can detect much fine work and some genius. But the passage of a few years will show more clearly which of them is to rank high and which of them we can disregard.

In what I have written, I have purposely avoided as far as I can the current jargon of art-literature, most of which seems to me neither an adornment of the English language nor to be in itself comprehensible.

Terms like "linear rhythm" or plastic value are but evasions of simpler phrases. I prefer to look upon sculpture from the point of view of the sculptors (as far as I can) with a sympathy which is bred of the most profound respect for an admiration of their art.

I am deeply indebted to many friends. To Carl Milles for the superb photographs which illustrate his work, but more for days in Stockholm that are not easily forgotten.

To Paul Manship for his many kindnesses and tolerant endurance of my many requests, here and in Paris. The photographs of his sculpture are all lent to me by him.

To Frank Dobson I own the admirable photographs of his work, taken by Mr EJ Mason, but most of all I am indebted to him for permission to reproduce his most recent, and as yet unknown work, the stone figure shown on Fig 31. It has indeed been a rare pleasure and a privilege to see his work in process of creation.

Eric Gill has done this little book the honour of a special design for the title page. Knowing of his sympathy with some of my views I can only thank him by expressing in the following chapters a few more which, I trust, meet with his assent!

I have to thank Messrs Bruckmann of Munich for the use of photographs of the work of Professor Georg Kolbe, and Professor Kolbe himself for the permission to use them.

Herr Oswald Herzog has allowed me photographs of his most interesting work through the medium of the Deutsche Kunstgemeinschaft in the Unter den Linden, Berlin.

By the Chanin Construction Company of New York I have been provided with the photographs of their attractive and successful sculptural decoration in the magnificent new Chanin Building.

To Messrs Arthur Tooth & Sons, I am indebted for the photographs of the work of Ossip Zadkine and to Mr F Lessore, proprietor of the Beaux Arts Gallery in Bruton Place, for the photograph of a torso by Mr Skeaping which I reproduce by the kindness of that artist.

Finally, my debt to M. Alexander Archipenjko is a large one, for he has lent me all photographs of his sculptures which appear here.

S.C.

Preface to "Progress of Archaeology" by Stanley Casson,

First published by G Bell & Sons, London in 1934.

The chapters of this book originally appeared as a series of articles in 1933 in the Listener. Certain additions and alterations have been made, but I am indebted to the Editor of the Listener and to the B.B.G. for permission to reproduce those articles.

My intention in this book is to make a survey of recent additions to archaeological knowledge and to the study of history made as a result of excavations carried out during the last twenty years. Most of the discoveries have, however, been made since the War.

I have made no attempt to mention all excavations — that would indeed be impossible in a book of this size, but I have tried to emphasise those regions where discovery has made the greatest strides and to concentrate on those particular discoveries which have made real additions to knowledge. I am fully conscious that there are many gaps and omissions and that students of archaeology will differ from me in the importance which I assign in some cases to special finds and particular areas.

But as far as possible I have tried to take a purely objective outlook on the present state of archaeological research, without letting my own particular interests prejudice my selection

I think it is safe to say that the last fifteen years has seen a great increase of archaeological research and a vast improvement in the methods of excavation.

I have done my best to pay my tribute to archaeological colleagues by thus attempting to explain to non-specialist readers the importance of their discoveries, above all by making clear the interrelation of areas and finds, where they are interrelated ; where there is no relation or connection between what at first sight seem to be related finds, it is equally important to emphasise the isolation of those areas or finds.

I have avoided technical archaeological terms as far as possible, and I have equally avoided, I hope, any attempt to ' popularise ' what, by its nature, is a study unsuitable for popularisation, in the accepted sense of that term.

S. C.

Oxford, 1934

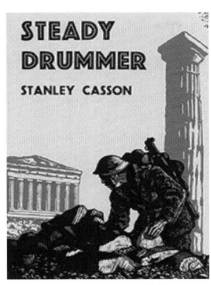

"Steady Drummer" by Stanley Casson

First published by G. Bell & Sons Ltd. (London, 1935).

Review by Lucy London

Front cover design of the original 1935 edition

The Original Publisher's advertisement:

"Mr. Stanley Casson is a well-known archaeologist and writer; in this book he appears as scholar and soldier. It is the uncompromising say of a survivor of the generation that was decimated in the War, stirred to speak by the recurrence of warlike activities and mentality.

The range of the book is wide; France, Salonika, Athens, Constantinople, Batum — all come within the orbit of the book; but the greater part deals with the Balkan campaign. The author maintains that this area should be looked on as the right flank of the long drawn-out allied line; when that flank was turned by the Bulgarian collapse, the first step towards winning the whole battle was achieved.

There is an interesting section on the 'forgotten war' in Turkestan, at the time when England was expensively supporting White Russia; and there is a poignant account of the erection of Rupert Brooke's memorial at Skyros.

The author's acquaintance as an archaeologist with the battlefields which were fought over by the ancient Greeks, and again in the Great War, gives a particular edge to a book that is never lacking in interest or irony."

The title of the book was inspired by this poem by A.E. Houseman (1859-1936):

"On the idle hill of summer"

On the idle hill of summer,
Sleepy with the flow of streams,
Far I hear the steady drummer
Drumming like a noise in dreams.

Far and near and low and louder
On the roads of earth go by,
Dear to friends and food for powder,
Soldiers marching, all to die.

East and west on fields forgotten
Bleach the bones of comrades slain,
Lovely lads and dead and rotten;
None that go return again.

Far the calling bugles hollo,
High the screaming fife replies,
Gay the files of scarlet follow:
Woman bore me, I will rise.

From "A Shropshire Lad" Poem No. 35: "On the idle hill of summer" BY A. E. HOUSMAN

Review of "Steady Drummer" by Lucy London

Having been told about Stanley Casson's book about his First World War experiences in France and Salonika by Jennifer MacLellan, I was given a copy for Christmas 2020.

Written and published during the 1930s, in "Steady Drummer", Casson tells us about his service in the East Lancashire Regiment on the Western Front, where he was wounded, and in Salonika, Macedonia on the Balkan Front.

It is an extremely interesting and very well written book and definitely one of the finest books about the conflict that I have read so far.

Casson has an honest and open way of describing the build up to the start of the war, the events he witnessed and the battles he took part in.   If you only read one book about WW1, I advise you to make it "Steady Drummer".

The cover shows a painting of the Fire of Salonika – a coloured reproduction of an aerial photograph taken at the time.

Casson's own words explain it better than I can, so here are a few extracts from "A Steady Drummer":

"The close of 1911 seemed to postpone the war indefinitely. … A strange play, *The Englishman's Home*, kept up our anticipations. Some hailed it as unadulterated nonsense, others as the great Apocalyptic warning. In fact it was the very first example of propaganda which was ever launched in our country." p. 16

Having signed up to join the Army as soon as war was declared, Stanley "...waited patiently for my country to answer the request which I had so dutifully made to it. But nobody seemed to be in a hurry, so for some weeks I was left with nothing to do but to read newspapers..." p. 23

"I was under no illusions whatever as to the nature of war. I had seen the traces of it in the Balkans, and I knew that our war would be far more unpleasant, if only because it would be waged with efficiency ..." p. 24

"In these post-war days I think that the outlook of the young men of 1914 requires some explanation, partly because so few of those young men have survived to explain, and partly because the young men of 1916 and 1917 and 1918 had wholly different problems to face and none of our pre-war knowledge to help them to face them. The reasons for becoming a soldier in 1917 or 1918 were totally different from the reasons that made us into soldiers." P. 48

Re Gallipoli: "Seldom in the war had 30 thousand men found themselves faced by 3 thousand...The value of surprise passed in a day, and the war was prolonged for nearly 2 years". p. 127.

In Chapter X, Stanley tells us about the Great Fire of Salonika: "That evening I walked along the sea-front towards G.H.Q. (General Head Quarters) and noticed that a house almost in the centre of the town had caught fire. No one seemed to be doing anything much, and I imagined that it would soon be burnt out.

Some cook, I was told, had upset a frying-pan full of oil, and the blaze had burned the house. As I walked along the front I watched the officers on leave dining with nurses in comfort and luxury in the open windows of the only large hotel.

... When I returned to walk back to my camp, I saw great sheets of flame rising from the heart of the city, with clouds of black smoke rising high and wide. ... Long flames were licking over to the very boats in the harbour against the quay and I saw several large fishing smacks burst into flame, with their sails afire, and break from their moorings to drift out to sea.

The city was burning in its very heart and there was no kind of organisation ready to save it." Pp. 184 – 185.

There is so much more – I could go on and on but I don't want to spoil your enjoyment of the book. Please read it.

Lucy London. May 2021

Preface to "Progress And Catastrophe" by Stanley Casson

Published by Harper & Brothers, New York & London in 1937

IN THIS small book I have attempted a single task- to search through the records of civilisation for those elements which lead to what is usually called Progress, and also for those elements which lead to the opposite movement, Retrogression.

Such elements are more easily perceived in the earlier stages of the development of mankind, so that my material lies in the main part in the field where the archaeologist is the best observer. The two great triumphs of Retrogression occurred, one in an age before the universal recording of history, the other when, by good fortune, fairly full records are available. I have, therefore, used the evidence available in each case, archaeological in the former, literary and archaeological in the latter.

I have tried faithfully to let the evidence tell its own story, and have commenced my analysis without any prepossessions. I do not believe that human history follows any pattern or shape, or that there are any known causes of rise or fall which are followed by predictable effects. Historical analogies are usually foolish and always dangerous and I have striven to avoid them.

But a study of the evidence reveal tendencies which follow more or less along well-defined grooves. To-day it seems of profound importance to study these tendencies and to see whether those which we can observe operative in the past are also operative in the present.

If we conclude that contemporary conditions suggest the reappearance of retrogressive forces we can at least try to arrest them and reverse the direction of disruptive tendencies. To that extent this book is a study in applied optimism rather than an admission of defeat.

Much that I have written is controversial. Many of my archaeological conclusions and critical comments are open to dispute. Many of my facts can be countered by other facts. But I hope that out of the general mass of evidence I have collected, it is at least possible for the reader to discern the main elements of human advance and human retirement.

Any general history of civilisation will give the material for a study such as this, but it seems to me that those who have written world histories have too often forgotten the earlier stages of man's development and stressed too much those periods which are most fully documented. In so doing they fail all too often to discover those tendencies which it is the purpose of this book to emphasise.

No scientific study can be of use to humanism unless it has an application to contemporary life. I have attempted to make such application from the study of archaeology, by producing examples which seem to have a value at the present day. I can only apologise for making a book which is little more than a series of conclusions about human history which deserve, more to-day than perhaps at any other time, the contemplation of the incurable optimist and the respect of the confirmed pessimist.

I am myself neither the one nor the other.

"Murder By Burial"
By Stanley Casson

First published by Hamish Hamilton
(London, 1938)
Reprinted by Penguin Books
(London, 1943 & 1946)

Review by Paul Breeze, June 2021

This is a delightful crime novel in an unusual setting and featuring very unusual characters. In view of the fact that the author Stanley Casson was by profession an archaeologist and academic, it is hard to imagine that the ideas in this book and the characters who act them out are not based to a certain extent on real people that he would have met during his travels and adventures.

In fact, Casson's daughter Jennifer MacLellan actually told us: "I think Death by Burial was written as a bit of a joke. A challenge perhaps as a result of his knowing Max Mallowan and Agatha Christie. He invented several detective stories for my bedtime story and I still remember bits of them."

The actual book is rather difficult to get hold of - having been out of print for over 70 years – although it is available on "Kindle" somewhere, apparently - so, as you are fairly unlikely ever to read it, I will tell you a bit about the plot.

Reading the story, it feels as if it is set in some sort of Miss Marple-esque country village but the place actually has its own cathedral so, therefore, must be somewhat bigger than that.

The Canon is keen on local history and wishes to excavate some public land to try and uncover traces of an important pre-Roman settlement.

There is also a rather potty retired army colonel who owns the neighbouring land who is also a keen amateur historian and feels he is competition with the Canon and wants to to shine a light on the Roman influences in the region and highlight what they did to bring civilisation to the area.

The Colonel has also set up his own private Roman Guard of local youths who he is planning to equip with illegally imported weapons smuggled in from the Spanish Civil War by some dubious associates. He has come up with the idea that he might need to fend off some sort of coup by a future socialist government who might want to dispossess all the rich landowners of their property, and needs to be ready for that eventuality.

Unlike a lot of murder mysteries where the crime happens at the beginning and the rest of the book features the ensuing investigation, in this case the murder doesn't come until a good half way through and, even then, it is not initially clear that it really was a murder.

Basically, the Canon gets buried when one the walls of his excavated trench collapses and he dies of a broken neck. It looks like an unfortunate accident until the local archeaological inspector turns up to have a routine look at the site and notices some irregularities in the artefacts that have been uncovered.

The Inspector has a brother who is an architect and he invites him to inspect the trench as none of the workmen on the site could work out why it should suddenly have caved in.

So, the Archaeologist, the Architect and the rather "spiffing" tweedy niece of the village doyen - who had been assisting the Canon with the dig - begin to suspect foul play and have to try and convince the local police to investigate.

This book is very much of its day – it was first published in 1938 – and reflects many of the values of the time. The class system is very much in evidence with everybody being deferential to the people of higher station and there is lots of tea and sherry being drunk at the appropriate times.

One thing that strikes me - as a modern day reader who never experienced life in pre WW2 Britain – are the fascinating styles of dialogue that Stanley uses throughout the book.

There are huge swathes of monologue which are, in fact, part of conversation where important aspects in the story are explored. But, rather than short bursts of interaction, they do seem to go on a bit and in some places it's quite difficult to realise that it is the same person doing the talking.

Now, we are talking intellectual people here and in the days before everybody had television and computers, I do appreciate that people used to talk more, so maybe that's just how things were...

The choice of language that Casson uses for the workers is quite noticeable too as he has them all sounding like - the best way I can describe it - is Jon Pertwee in Worzel Gummidge.

The manual labourers on the archaeological dig and even the Police Sergeant all say things like "Oi knows that for a faaact, oi does..."

I haven't a clue what people in rural Suffolk – or wherever the story is supposed to be set - actually used to talk like back in those days but, as Stanley Casson spent some time living in that area, I daresay he knows what he is talking about.

Elsewhere, the otherwise very correct and respectable (and middle class) Police Inspector refers to the Italians as "Wops" at one point and the potty Colonel's butler sounds rather like Parker out of Thunderbirds in his manner of speaking. By this I mean, he adds an "h" at the start of words where they shouldn't be one and drops it where there should be one, ie: "I ham 'appy to h-oblige...", or whatever.

This in itself is a very interesting point and was obviously a widespread thing at the time. Casson actually put a footnote to the text to explain this, saying:

"Butlers' aspirates are employed irrationally. In dialects the aspirate appears or disappears according to fixed rules."

So there you are: a fascinating look at social history from the Britain of the 1930s and a really enjoyable crime mystery novel all at the same time. On the off chance that you ever get hold of a copy of "Murder by Burial", I would heartily recommend you give it a read!

Dust cover illustration to the original
Hamish Hamilton edition of Murder by Burial

PREFACE to "The Discovery Of Man – The Story Of The Inquiry Into Human Origins" by Stanley Casson.

First published by Hamish Hamilton, London, in 1939

IN writing this book I had no intention of writing a history of the twin studies of Archaeology and Anthropology. That would only be possible in a work consisting of several large volumes.

My intention rather was to sketch the outlines of a single story — the story of how Man has come to be studied objectively.

In all sciences there is a series of stages of development. First comes simple curiosity, stimulated sometimes by practical needs and demands. Then comes the organisation of the ways in which that vague curiosity is to be applied. Next appears the organisation of results, and finally the growth of a properly conducted method of inquiry.

What I have attempted to do is to illustrate those stages of development as they concern the two studies with which this book deals. Sometimes a scientific study or a branch of learning remains for a long time in an undeveloped stage of growth. Then some acute mind appears, some man of vision and brilliance, who by his contributions advances that study to a new and more developed condition.

My purpose in writing this book has been to describe the growth of the two branches of learning with which it deals from this point of view only.

I have emphasised the work done by certain particular men, and have necessarily omitted mention of the work of hundreds of other minor men whose contributions in the aggregate are important, but whose individual work has not necessarily advanced the subject. That is why it has never been my intention to make a mere catalogue of achievement.

Instead I have given an outline of the growth of the subject as a whole and paused at those moments when really epoch-making contributions have been made by men of genius. More than that could not be done in one volume.

History, as we are only too well aware in these days, is made by individuals. Science and learning and scholarship are also dependent on individual work. Men of the stature of Newton, Darwin, and Einstein have revolutionised the studies which they pursued. Without them the development of those studies would have followed a slower progress, or might even have remained static.

Great scholars and scientists serve as a stimulus to countless others of less calibre. Without the greater men the less might not even exist.

The story of the slow realisation that Man is as suitable a subject for objective study as any other organism is a strange and fascinating tale. The conquering of his innate prejudices is one part of it, and his triumphant realisation of his origins is another.

The discovery of how he succeeded in creating civilisation out of primitive chaos is a subsidiary tale the more exciting because its outlines have only so recently been told.

S.C. Oxford

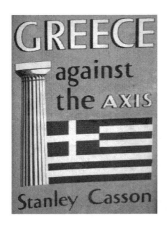

"Greece Against The Axis" by Stanley Casson

Published by Hamish Hamilton, (London, 1941)

In his Preface, Casson explains:

The following pages are an attempt to give at first hand a general impression of the campaign in Greece in which the Greek nation defeated the grandiose Italian attempt at invasion and occupation of Greece and fought to the bitter end against the savage attack launched by the full force of the German army and air force. This book is published with the permission of the War Office which is, of course, not responsible for any expressions of opinion found herein.

My story is a story of the greatest catastrophe which has ever overwhelmed the Greek people and Greece itself. I have drawn the main outlines of a tragedy. But the tragedy is one in three parts, like the ancient trilogies of Greek drama. Part I is the tragedy of Italy. Part II is the tragedy of Greece. Part III has not yet been played. In it the avenging furies will take the leading part.

I have made no attempt to give a detailed military outline of the events of the campaign in proper sequence. At this stage of the Second World War, full details are neither available nor desirable.

All I have attempted and wanted to do is to give to my readers an account of what took place in Greece and on its borders during those agonising 6 months in which Greece showed an example in the world of heroism and integrity which has never yet been equalled in her long history.

The full military history of the campaign will no doubt be compiled later.

Review by Paul Breeze (October 2021)

Most books about the Second World War that we read are written from the modern day perspective and with the benefit of hindsight, ie we all know it finished. But at the time that Stanley was writing his book about the Greek campaign, it was far from finished, and at the time of his premature death in an air crash April 1944, his beloved Greece was still under Nazi occupation.

In order that you can understand the full historical context of what Stanley is writing about in this book, there is a useful potted history of the Axis occupation of Greece on the Wikipedia website, which reads as follows:

"The occupation of Greece by the Axis Powers began in April 1941 after Nazi Germany invaded the Kingdom of Greece to assist its ally, Fascist Italy, which had been at war with Allied Greece since October 1940. Following the conquest of Crete, all of Greece was occupied by June 1941.

The occupation of the mainland lasted until Germany and its ally Bulgaria were forced to withdraw under Allied pressure in early October 1944.

However, German garrisons remained in control of Crete and some other Aegean islands until after the end of World War II in Europe, surrendering these islands in May and June 1945.

Fascist Italy had initially declared war and invaded Greece in October 1940, but the Hellenic Army managed to push back the invading forces into neighbouring Albania, then an Italian protectorate. Nazi Germany intervened on its ally's behalf in southern Europe.

While most of the Hellenic Army was located on the Albanian front to fend off the relentless Italian counter-attacks, a rapid German Blitzkrieg campaign commenced in April 1941, and by June (with the conquest of Crete) Greece was defeated and occupied.

The Greek government went into exile, and an Axis collaborationist puppet government was established in the country. Greece's territory was divided into occupation zones run by the Axis powers, with the Germans administering the most important regions of the country themselves, including Athens, Thessaloniki and the strategic Aegean Islands. Other regions of the country were given to Germany's partners, Italy and Bulgaria."

Now, I have to say that Casson's book is absolutely FASCINATING and while it is, obviously, about an unfortunate subject, he goes about it in a really positive and entertaining fashion and, once I started reading it, I could not put the book down.

What I especially like about this book is, despite the fact that it is written by a professional archaeologist and university tutor, it is not in any way stuffy or pompous or condescending - but is very easy to read and written in a very personal and informative manner.

In terms of looking back at World War 2 overall, most modern day people actually know very little about the Greek campaign – other than possibly what they might have gleaned from Hollywood films such as "Captain Corelli's

Mandolin" and "The Guns of Navarone" - so this book is a welcome bit of reality written straight from the heart of somebody who clearly cares deeply about the region and its people.

The book starts with Casson's arrival in Greece in November 1940, just after the Italian army had launched an invasion attempt on the country from its bases in neighbouring Albania, which Italian dictator Mussolini had annexed by force in 1939.

The plucky Greeks successfully repelled the invasion and forced the Italians back deep into Albanian territory. Unfortunately, this failure to secure the whole of the Balkans for the Axis Powers (Bulgaria and Rumania were already allied to Germany) made it more likely that the Nazis would attack and finish the job.

Casson explains that with Germans planning to invade the Soviet Union in June 1941, (which nobody except them actually knew about until it happened...) they needed to be sure that there was no chance of a counter attack by the Allies on their flank coming through the Balkans, which is why this move was so important.

During the First World War, British troops based in Salonika in northern Greece had been able to drive a wedge between the armies of the Central Powers which contributed to their failure in the region back then - and the Germans were keen to not let this happen again.

Casson's mission as a member of the Intelligence Corps in Greece was to travel around and survey the likely points for a German attack, assess the terrain and devise defensive strategies. He looked at roads and bridges and identified where construction works needed doing to allow British reinforcements to gain access to where they would be needed to bolster the Greek forces.

Casson was well suited to this role as he knew Greece very well – both from his time there as a soldier during the First World War and also from his many years there working as an archaeologist and tutor at the British School in Athens.

Now, if you can possibly try and set aside the fact that this book was written in the middle of a war - with thousands of people being killed and subjugated across the globe – it actually comes across as a rather charming travelogue.

He describes the route he took on his circular journey around Greece and goes into delightful detail about the towns and villages that he stopped in. He tells of the historical significance of many of the places and how they were the sites of famous battles in Ancient Greece.

He talks about the countryside, the views, the rivers, the mountains, the architecture and the people in the different areas and you can tell that he has a deep and genuine love for this country.

However, when it comes to describing the enemy, he does not mince his words and expresses opinions that in our modern day "touchy feely" society some people might find shocking to hear. But you have to remember the frightening times that this book was written in – and that it was, to all intents and purposes, a propaganda book – albeit a nice one.

He is very uncomplimentary about the Italians' abilities as soldiers and most disdainful about Mussolini's claims that all Italians were descended from pure Roman stock.

He calls the Bulgarians "half savages" and refers to the fact that they had also attacked Greece during the First World War on the orders of their German masters - and had carried out numerous other cross border atrocities in previous Balkan conflicts.

He describes Germans as sinister and bullying – among lots of other unsavoury things – and writes off all Teutons as deluded criminal types.

Casson also mentions the duplicitous way that the Germans behaved during the build up to the invasion with their Minister in Athens making speeches about peace, and his wife visiting Greek war casualties in hospitals, while all the while their troops were amassing in holding camps across the border in Bulgaria ready to mount an attack.

The second half of the book deals with the invasion by the Germans and the eventual fall back of the Allied forces, who have to be evacuated by ship after a series of brave defensive stands. It is very well written and entertaining to read and the detail that Casson goes into is superb.

So there you are. If you'd like to know a bit more serious background to the conflict that was covered in those Hollywood films that I mentioned earlier – or, indeed, those less well remembered such as the one where Dirk Bogarde is sent to kidnap a German general and has to escape through the mountains, then this is the book for you.

If you can find a copy ....!

Casson was never actually a professional soldier – he was by profession an archaeologist and academic - and he only ever donned uniform in time of war to answer the call of his country.

Nestled away in this book about Greece he explains his own philosophy thus:

Personally, I can hardly endure to see troops marching in war because I have seen so many, and that marching of troops emphasises the folly of war only too clearly!

> "East and West on fields forgotten
> Lie the bones of comrades slain;
> Lovely lads – and dead and rotten:
> None that go return again"

That may sound like pacifism but it also happens to be war. My own attitude to war has never varied. It is that of the French soldier who wrote:

"Je haïs tellemement la guerre qui j'ai l'intention de la subir toute entièrement!"

That, incidentally, is why I happen to be a soldier now.

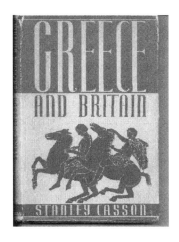

"Greece And Britain" by Stanley Casson

Published by Collins
(London, 1943)

Review by Paul Breeze (October 2021)

Let me start off here by saying that I have learned – or at least understood – considerably more about British history and, indeed, the ancient Greeks, from reading this book by Stanley Casson than I ever did from years of being told about it at school.

Now, I don't know if that is because I am now older and can assimilate information more easily – or at least in a different way. Maybe I am just receptive to more varied things now than I was when I was 7 or 8 or 12, I don't really know. But my guess is that it is mainly down to the way that the information has been presented.

I recall that, at school, we had interminably boring history classes about burial mounds, bits of bronze age helmets and spears that had been dug up, triremes (to throw in another random word that I remember from those days…) and all sorts other things that I fully acknowledge may well have been very interesting, had they been handled differently, or, dare I say, explained to me by Stanley Casson!

From reading Casson's book, I have learned for the first time that Lord Byron was a prime figure in the Greeks' battle for independence from Turkey in the 1820s and that he died of malaria while based over there actively supporting the armed conflict.

I have also discovered that the famous "Elgin Marbles" are not, in fact, "marbles" at all but a collection of fine ancient Greek marble statues that were pilfered during one of Greece's low periods of history when it was merely a poor province under Turkish rule – continuing a trend that had started with the Roman Conquest of much of Europe when historical sites were routinely ransacked.

And that there was also a collection of "Arundel Marbles" somewhat cynically acquired in the 1600 and 1700s by the Earl of Arundel.

I now also know where Carthage used to be - and that it was ancient Greek traders who first settled the Mediterranean port of Marseilles.

What I find interesting – and most enjoyable - about this book, is that Stanley charts the history of the relationship between Greece and Britain with stories of people rather than just "things".

He starts off many centuries BC with the early explorations of the Minoans from Crete and the Phoenecians and early Greeks who gradually found their way out of the Mediterranean and up along the coastlines of what we know today as Portugal and France eventually finding their way north to our shores.

And he looks at how traders were first attracted to the British Isles due to the rich tin reserves that were being mined in Cornwall and along the south coast.

And how this was an important component in the making of the bronze that they used to manufacture their weapons.

He tells the fascinating story of sea captain and astronomer Pytheas of Marseilles, who sailed to Britain in around 325 BC, circumnavigated much of the British Isles and then proceeded to get as far as Scandinavia.

He explains the founding of Byzantium and the transition of Constantinople in a way that is easy to follow and does the same with the succession of ancient Britons, Celts and Saxons who peopled our own islands before the respective conquests by the Romans and Normans.

Jumping ahead slightly, there is a fascinating account of a visit to Britain during the reign of Henry VIII by Greek adventurer Nicander Nucius and also the tale of Englishman John Dallam who travelled to Greece around 1600.

Recent history has seen Britain as a powerful ally to Greece. The whole region of the Balkans was subjugated by the Turkish Ottoman Empire for much of its later history and Britain was one of its key allies in its push for independence in the 1820s. British forces were deployed to Greece in the First World War to help fight off Bulgarian aggression and an Expeditionary Force was also rushed to the Balkans to support their efforts in the face of invasion by Italy and Germany during World War 2. And Casson knows all about that as he was in the thick of things in both of those conflicts.

So this book really just about covers it all.

It is beautifully illustrated with 11 coloured plates of paintings of areas of Greece from different periods and over 60 black and white drawings and photos that help tell the story.

Illustrations from "Greece And Britain" (the original book plates are in colour...)

Top: The Siege Of Athens During The Greek War Of Independence 1821-1828 (ca. 1830s)
Gouache by Panagiotis Zographos especially drawn for General Makryjannis.

Bottom: The French Consul At Athens - Coloured engraving by Louis Dupre (1789-1837)
(Shows one of the marbles later brought to England by Lord Elgin.)

A Lost Hero Of The Authors' Club - by CJ Schüler

Entering Waterstones' Gower Street branch in central London the other day, I came face to face with a shelving bay full of old green Penguin crime novels.

In the centre, at eye level, I was intrigued and delighted to find a battered copy of Stanley Casson's *Murder by Burial*. Casson was a member of the Authors' Club, and this 1938 murder mystery was a one-off jeu d'esprit by a distinguished archaeologist and authority on Ancient Greek sculpture, of whom I became aware while researching the Club's history.

During the First World War, Casson fought with the East Lancashire Regiment in Flanders, where he was wounded in 1915. He then served on the General Staff in Salonika, and was mentioned in dispatches and awarded the Greek Order of the Saviour.

After the war, he became Assistant Director of the British School at Athens, and in 1920 took up a Fellowship at New College, Oxford.

On his arrival in the quadrangle, the Warden, William Archibald Spooner (who contributed an -ism to the language), invited him to lunch 'to welcome Stanley Casson, our new archaeology Fellow'. 'But Warden,' he said, 'I *am* Stanley Casson.' 'Never mind,' Spooner replied. 'Come all the same.'

Casson's tastes were eclectic. His many publications ranged from *The Technique Of Early Greek Sculpture* (1933) through 'Byzantium and Anglo-Saxon Sculpture' to *Some Modern Sculptors*, a 1929 survey of the art from Rodin to Epstein – whom he, unlike some of his Authors' Club colleagues, admired. One of his students at Oxford was Max Mallowan, the archaeologist who went on to marry Agatha Christie.

When war was declared in 1939, Casson joined the Intelligence Corps with the rank of Lieutenant Colonel, and became an instructor at the Intelligence Training Centre in Matlock, Derbyshire.

Among his pupils there was a young second lieutenant who shared his passion for Hellenic culture, and with whom he always conversed in Greek. His name was Patrick Leigh Fermor. Casson was setting up a military mission to his beloved Greece, to which he recruited Fermor, who would subsequently capture the commander of the German forces on Crete, General Heinrich Kreipe. In 1942, Casson published *Greece Against the Axis*, his eye-witness account of the Italian and German invasions of that country in 1940–41.

In February 1944 Casson, along with Graham Greene, was invited to join the Authors' Club's executive committee. Before the next meeting, however, the club was shocked to learn that he had been killed in a plane crash off the coast of Cornwall while flying to Cairo on active service.

The committee commissioned his widow to compile a memorial bibliography of his works, and once the war was over, on 29 November 1945, held a reception with the Anglo-Hellenic League at the Dorchester, at which tributes were paid to his life and work, and a collection was raised to fund a library of English books in Greece.

C.J. Schüler's Writers, Lovers, Soldiers, Spies: A History of the Authors' Club of London, 1891–2016, *is published by the Authors' Club, rrp. £19.99*

www.cjschuler.com

DEATH IN MYSTERIOUS CIRCUMSTANCES

Stanley Casson was killed in the early hours of 17th April 1944 when the RAF transport plane that he flying on crashed into the sea off Cornwall shortly after take-off.

He had been on his way to Greece on an SOE intelligence mission to pave the way for the eventual liberation of Greece and the other passengers on the flight were also intelligence staff and SOE personnel heading off to various destinations.

The circumstances surrounding the loss of the aircraft are rather mysterious so we thought it worth a closer look.

Compiled by Paul Breeze
From a variety of sources, including
https://www.ipswichwarmemorial.co.uk
www.carpentersco.com

THE AIRCREW

The 525 Squadron members who perished in this accident were:

RCAF Flying Officer Arthur Douglas Gavel - Pilot
RAFVR Flight Sergeant Michael Kingston Rowe - Co-pilot
RAFVR Flying Officer Albert George Tracey Gardiner - Navigator
RCAF Flying Officer Harold Calven Austen - Wireless operator / air gunner

Arthur Douglas Gavel (1921-1944)
Flying Office , Royal Canadian Air Force

Arthur Douglas Gavel was from Swift Current, Saskatchewan, in Canada. He was born on 12th February 1921 and his parents were George William Gavel and Vera Bell (Campbell) Gavel.

He joined the Royal Canadian Air Force in 1941 having previously been a Cadet in the Swift Current Cadet Corps, a Trooper in the 14th Canadian Light Horse (a local militia unit) and a Cadet at the University of Saskatchewan COTC

After going through flight training, he received his pilot's badge on 13th March 1942. He started off doing transatlantic flights, delivering new planes to Britain and was later transferred to RAF Moreton-in Marsh, from where he shipped Wellington bombers to the Middle East.

In September 1943, Gavel was drafted into the newly formed 525 RAF Squadron to fly transport services from the United Kingdom to Maison Blanche, Algiers, and United Kingdom to Malta.

In April of 1944, he was the Captain and Pilot of the Vickers Warwick I (BV247) flight that was to end in tragedy and mystery.

Michael Kingston Rowe (1922-1944)
Royal Air Force Volunteer Reserve
Flight Sergeant (Co-Pilot)
Michael Kingston Rowe was the son of Walter Stanley and Dorothy Florence Rowe, of Kingston-on-Thames, Surrey.

Flight Sergeant Rowe, although not an acknowledged regular crewman, he had flown previously with Arthur Gavel. He body was also initially missing on the morning of the crash but was eventually recovered from the sea on the 8th May, within the general area of the crash.

Flying Officer Albert George Tracey Gardiner (1917-1944)
Royal Air Force Volunteer Reserve
Flying Officer (Navigator)

Born in June 1917 in Dorking, Surrey, England, Albert George Tracey Gardiner was the son of William T. Gardiner (1889-1951) and Ruth Mary Greenaway (1889-1951) and brother to Rosemary Muriel Gardiner (1918-2001) and Evelyn B. Gardiner (1920-1999). Sadly, little else is known about him

Harold Calven Austen (1918-1944),
Royal Canadian Air Force
Flying Officer (Wireless Operator / Air Gunner)

Born on August 15, 1918 in Oyen, Alberta, Canada, Flying Officer Austen was the son of Henry John Austen (1892–1956) and Mary Alice (Gibson) Austen (1886–1922) of Oyen, Alberta, Canada. At the age of 22, he enlisted on May 21, 1941 in Edmonton, Alberta. Prior to his enlistment he had been employed as a mechanic.

THE PASSENGERS

The plane carried twelve passengers, of whom three were members of 525 Squadron travelling as passengers on the way to overseas postings. These were:

RAF Squadron Leader William Godfrey Tiley;
RAFVR Flying Officer Noel Spencer Nicklin
and RAF Pilot Officer George William Lamb.

William Godfrey Tiley
RAF Squadron Leader

Born in Colerne, Wiltshire, England, February 27, 1910 the son of William Tilley (1872-1952) and Emma Selina (Holder) Tilley (1884-1966). He was the brother of Jocelyn Richard James Tilley (1921-2002) and Joyce Marguerite Tilley (1912-1918).

He had been in the RAF for over 17 years. From May 22, 1941 to July 18, 1943, he was with 31 OTU (Operational Training Unit) at Debert, Nova Scotia first with the rank of Flight Lieutenant, and later as Squadron Leader.

George William Lamb (1916-1944)
Royal Air Force
Pilot Officer

Born 9th August 1916, Pilot Officer Lamb was the son of William Saunders Lamb and Jeannie Noble (Byth) Lamb of Hull and husband of Doreen Alice (Wilson) Lamb of Hull.

Noel Spencer Nicklin (1919-1944)

Royal Air Force Volunteer Reserve Flying Officer

Born 19th December 1909, Flying Officer Nicklin was the son of Frederick William and Selina (Spenser) Nicklin of Waterloo, Liverpool. According to the Natwestgroupmembers website, he was educated at Merchant Taylors' School, Crosby, and joined the staff of Westminster Bank at its Liverpool Waterloo branch in December 1926. Over the next 15 years he spent time working in the bank's branches at Seaforth, Blackburn, Aigburth, Warrington and Lymm. Outside work he was a keen amateur magician.

In 1941 Nicklin left the Lymm branch to go on war service, becoming a Flying Officer in the Royal Air Force Volunteer Reserve. In addition to his conventional duties, he used his magic skills to entertain at military hospitals and camps and organised concert parties for troops.

Alongside Stanley Casson, the other passengers were:-

Lieutenant Colonel Ivor Watkins BIRTS, (SOE Yugoslavia) (1910-1944)

Lt Col Ivor Watkins Birts was born in 1910 in Kensington, the son of William Thomas Watkins Birts, Senior Warden of the Carpenters' Company in 1941 and his wife Lilian (nee Stephens).

He became a Freeman and Liveryman of the Carpenters' Company in 1931. He took a B.A. at Merton College, Oxford and qualified as a Barrister, but later practiced as a stockbroker. He married Josephine Bain in 1934 and had two children, Carol and Douglas.

On the outbreak of war he joined the Royal Artillery, serving at Larkhill, Salisbury Plain and South Eastern Command, Home Forces.

He was promoted to Captain in 1941 and Major in 1942. He was posted to General Head Quarters in Cairo with MO4, the Middle East and Balkans branch of the Special Operations Executive (SOE) and subsequently in Eritrea.

In November 1943 he was promoted to Lieutenant Colonel as GSO 1 (General Staff Officer Rank 1) and served with Force 133, a subsidiary SOE headquarters in Bari, Southern Italy under Cairo, set up to control operations in the Balkans and Northern Italy and support the Greek and Yugoslav resistance movements.

(Biography from www.carpentersco.com)

RAF Air Commodore George Lionel Seymour DAWSON-DAMER (1907-1944) was Viscount CARLOW, the son of the 6th Earl of Portarlington.

According to the emocourt.net website, about his family's Emo Court estate in Ireland, Viscount Carlow was a gifted and versatile man who spoke 9 languages and was interested in sailing, foreign travel, book collecting and printing.

In 1936, Viscount Carlow founded the Corvinus Press in London. Only 58 titles were produced, and only five in editions of more than 100 copies.

He was a close friend of TE Lawrence and Carlow was at his deathbed in 1935.

He had previously been in command of 600 Squadron Auxiliary Air Force and had been a Grenadier Guards officer pre-war. Viscount Carlow was commissioned as a pilot officer in the Auxiliary Air Force in 1931.

As an accomplished pilot, he led a London based RAF squadron, but when World War II began, he was posted to the Intelligence section of the Air Ministry rather than to flying duties.

This work sent him on diplomatic missions to Finland, Portugal, Brazil, and Venezuela and he was en route to visit Tito in Yugoslavia.

With his knowledge of languages, he was probably the "Russian speaking MI6 operative" who was among the passengers on his way to Yugoslavia.

Kapitan Edmund Gojski
Polish Army
(1907-1944)

Gojski was born on 25th July 1907 at Skarżysko-Kamienna, which at the time was part of Congress Poland, under Russian control.

Poland's national borders were re-established at the end of the First World War after centuries of partitions and, in the 1930s, Edmund was serving in the Polish army as a Lieutenant in the Budslaw Border Protection Battalion, on the border with the Soviet Union.

In the Summer of 1939, the battalion formed a Reconnaissance company and when Polish troops were mobilised after the German invasion on 1st September 1939, Gojski was drawn into the newly formed 207 infantry regiment (Krasne Battalion) as their recon officer. He was involved in the defence of Lvov against the Soviets after they attacked the country from the East on 17th September 1939.

We are not quite sure what he did next but he is bound to have had quite a few scrapes and adventures evading the Russians and Germans before ending up in England in April 1944 ready to fly back to still occupied Poland as a courier.

Major Jozef Krol, Senior Chaplain Polish Forces (1906-1944)

Fr. Józef Król was born on 21st March 1906 in the village of Ignacówka near Jędrzejów in the Kielce region.

His parents, Andrzej and Rozalia née Marcinkowski were farmers and they had 9 sons and 2 daughters.

Józef was ordained as a priest in 1933 and went on to work in Vilnius and Jazno at the very north-eastern edge of Poland.

He was appointed a military chaplain on 24th August 24 1939 and was involved in the defensive campaigns throughout September.

Krol crossed the Rumanian border with retreating Polish troops and was held in an internment camp for several months. From there he escaped and through Yugoslavia and Italy he got to France, where units of the Polish army were gathering.

When the Germans attacked Norway on 9th April 1940, the Allies sent an expeditionary corps to help the Norwegians, including Polish exiled troops – accompanied by Chaplain Krol. Following the British withdrawal he spent time back in England chaplaining the Polish forces in exile.

After the German attack on Russia in 1941 and the signing of the Polish-Soviet pact, Krol travelled with the employees of the new Polish embassy under construction to Moscow, and then to the re-organising Polish Army in Kyrgyzstan and Uzbekistan.

After spending time in the Middle East, Krol was sent back to Britain again to chaplain the Polish troops but he was desperate to go back to Poland and help his people - who were suffering executions and massacres - and to support the brave efforts of the Home Army.

He was eventually given permission to travel back to his homeland in an undercover capacity and undertook parachute training.

The two Poles were to fly initially to Gibraltar and then to Bari in Italy - another stepping stone in a complicated journey from where they were eventually to be dropped by parachute into occupied Poland.

(Additional Biographical information from https://archibial.pl/czas/arch30/art/krahel.htm)

Lieutenant Stephen Maitland (1911-1944)
Special Operations Executive (SOE) Lieutenant, British Army

Stephen Mate was born on 20th August 1911 in Kurd, Tolna, Hungary the son of Ferenz Mait (1889-1970) and Maria (Horvath) Mait. He was the brother of Rozalia Mate (Matyasovszky) (1922-2005) and Marie Mate.

Ferenz Mait moved to Ontario, Canada, in 1927 and the family joined him two years later when Stephen was eighteen.

Stephen enlisted in the Canadian Army on 28th August 28, 1942 at Port Arthur, Ontario. However, as he was fluent in both the English and Hungarian languages he was accepted for training with British Security Co-ordination (BSC).

He began training at Camp X for service with the Special Operations Executive (SOE) and, following three months' training, he was transferred to England in October 1943 and given a new identity as Lt. Stephen Maitland.

Maitland was en-route to Hungary via Brindisi in Italy on an SOE mission when he took off on the fateful flight from Cornwall.

Thomas Percival Ward on the occasion of his marriage to film actress Dorice Bentley Gunn in December 1931 (Leeds Mercury, 11ᵗʰ Dec 1931)

Major Thomas Percival WARD (1908-1944)

Royal Army Medical Corps

Born in 1908, Thomas Percival Ward was the son of Thomas Ward (1872-1949) and Alice Josephine Ward (1888-1970)

He was educated at Cambridge and St. Thomas College. He obtained degrees: M.A., M.B., B.Ch. (Cantab.). L.R.C.P., M.R.C.S.

During World War II he served with the Royal Army Medical Corps. He is commemorated on the St. Thomas Hospital Kings College (London)'s War Memorial.

Roger Achille Albert Baudouin (1896-1944)

Commander

Free French Forces

Baudouin was born on 6th November 1896. He had distinguished himself as a young Lieutenant in World War I and was decorated with the Croix de Guerre and awarded a Chevalier de la Légion d'Honneur.

Between the wars, he became a specialist in cryptography and gained a worldwide reputation

In June 1940, he left France to join General de Gaulle in London and worked with MI6 and the British Government Communications Headquarters at Bletchley Park with the decoding services, where he worked with Alan Turing.

Baudoin was promoted to Commander in 1943 and he was involved with Operation Fortitude – which was the code name for the military deception employed during the build-up to the 1944 Normandy landings to make the Germans believe that the landing would take place in Pas-de-Calais and not in Normandy.

As a passenger on the flight he was travelling from London to Algiers carrying documents to meet with General De Gaulle.

Maurice Schwob (1897-1944)
Free French Government Agent

Maurice Schwob was born on 20th July 1897 in Paris, France, the son Leon and Helena Schwob. He married Marjorie Stralem in New York in December 1925 and the couple had two daughters - Anne Marie and Diane Helene.

Prior to the outbreak of World War II, Maurice Schwob was an industrialist and merchant and travelled extensively, including visits to France, England, Switzerland, China (Shanghai), Canada, and the United States.

During World War II he served as a Free French Government Agent and travelled to the United States, Australia, Canada, and the Pacific.

On April 17, 1944 he was travelling from London to Algiers carrying documents to meet with General De Gaulle in Algiers.

*****

The details of the crash and subsequent investigation (or cover up as is suggested...) have been researched by the Wartime Heritage Association, who are based in Nova Scotia, Canada - which is where the pilot Arthur Gavel came from and where his brother still lives.

They have very kindly given us permission us to reproduce their article in full on the following pages.

You can also read lots more fascinating stories on their website at www.wartimeheritage.com

A Vickers Warwick C Mark I transport plane of the same type that Casson was killed on in April 1944. This aircraft is serial number BV256. Casson's was BV247 (Photo by Ministry of Aircraft Production)

Mystery Flight
Royal Air Force Squadron 525
Vickers Warwick C Mark I, BV247

Wartime Heritage Association
www.wartimeheritage.com

525 RAF Squadron Vickers Warwick C Mark I, BV247 was one of fourteen Warwick transports converted for use by British Overseas Airways Corporation (BOAC) and reverted to the Royal Air Force in September 1943.

The Squadron operated on routes throughout Europe and was mainly manned by Canadian personnel. The usual base of the aircraft BV247 was Asmera in Ethiopia (now Eritrea) where Squadron 525 also had a secondary base.

The flight of BV247, a scheduled service flight from the United Kingdom to Maison Blanche airport, Algiers, via Gibraltar, began on April 15, 1944.

The point of departure was RAF Transport Command's main base at RAF Station Lyneham in Wiltshire. After a routine air-test, 1680 lbs. of freight were loaded, and in the late afternoon twelve passengers boarded for the first leg of the flight to RAF Station St Mawgan, the overseas departure point in Cornwall.

The aircraft with a crew of four and twelve passengers departed RAF Station Lyneham in the late afternoon.

The crew of 525 Squadron: RCAF Flying Officer Arthur Douglas Gavel (Pilot); RAFVR Flight Sergeant Michael Kingston Rowe (2nd Pilot); RAFVR Flying Officer Albert George Tracey Gardiner (Navigator); and RCAF Flying Officer Harold Calven Austen (Wireless Operator/Air Gunner).

The routine for overseas flights was that unarmed transport aircraft would position at St Mawgan during daylight and await darkness before proceeding further - the purpose being to use the cover of darkness for that part of the journey down through the Bay of Biscay, and so hopefully avoid German fighters that ranged out from bases in occupied France.

In the late afternoon of April 15, 1944, Warwick BV247 arrived at St Mawgan. The scheduled time for take-off on the second leg of the flight (St Mawgan to Gibraltar) was in the early hours of 16 April 1944, but because of adverse weather, the flight was postponed for 24 hours.

The aircraft, with its cargo in locked cargo-holds, was left parked on dispersal at Green Site, on the St Mawgan Village side of the airfield, guarded by fixed sentries and dog-patrols, whilst crew and passengers went into transit-accommodation.

The re-scheduled time for the Warwick's departure was the early hours of April 17, 1944, and it was one of several aircraft scheduled to leave that night (April 16/17) for such places as Lisbon, Gibraltar, the Azores, Maison Blanche, Malta, Cairo, and India.

The passengers for BV247 checked in at the Despatch Office at about midnight and according to the rule for take-offs out over the sea, were fitted with Mae Wests [life jackets]. Passengers and crew were then bussed across the blacked-out airfield to Green site, and the Despatch Officer supervised their embarkation and the re-loading of their hand-luggage.

Then as a final task, he [the Despatch Officer] handed over to the pilot, Flying Officer Arthur Gavel, two Secret Mail Bags (SM18 and SM19). The bags had been delivered to St Mawgan Despatch Office late on the afternoon of April 16, 1944, with instructions that they were for conveyance to Maison Blanche - by the "safe hands of the pilot" of Warwick BV247.

The conveyance of diplomatic, departmental, and secret mail bags by the "safe hands of pilots" of transport aircraft had been agreed between the Foreign Office and the Air Ministry, and although it was not a regular routine it was an occasional requirement which pilots were conversant with and didn't question.

The pilot of the Warwick expressed his intention of carrying them up-front in his stowage compartment, and with that the cabin door was closed and the aircraft prepared to leave.

At 0004 hrs. GMT 17 April 1944, Warwick BV247 (Code DNY-A) was given the 'green' for take-off on St Mawgan's new main runway - on a heading straight out over the sea. A good lift-off was observed by the airfield controller in the caravan at the 32 end of the runway. The aircraft came unstuck at the intersection of runways 19 and 32. Climb-out was perfectly normal and he watched until navigation lights were routinely switched off, and then went about his other duties.

Everything was perfectly normal until the Warwick reached a height of approximately 2000 feet, and then at a point about a mile off the coast (still in line with the end of the runway), a Home Guard Sergeant saw an explosion, and the aircraft going down. He immediately reported what he had seen.

At day break, a total of fourteen bodies were recovered from the sea immediately below the position where the explosion had been observed, and plotted, by the Home Guard Sergeant.

Missing on the morning of the crash were the Pilot, Arthur Gavel, and the Second Pilot, Michael Rowe. Their bodies were recovered in the following weeks.

The body of Arthur Gavel was recovered on Whipsiderry Beach on April 25th and the body of Michael Rowe was recovered from the sea off Watergate on May 8th.

A Court of Inquiry was convened within 48 hours but failed to consider all evidence available. The report concluded that factors contributing to the incident were "not known".

The mystery of what happened to the flight of Vickers Warwick C Mark I, BV247 has lingered for years. It began, first, as a result of the recovery of bodies and debris the following morning. *"The crews of the rescue boats soon realized that the Warwick had not been engaged on a routine transport flight; a body- belt recovered from the sea by the Lifeboat Mechanic was found to contain $69,000 in press packed $100 bills, sewn into pouches around the belt; a small suitcase recovered [...] was found to contain £45,000 brand new £5 Bank of England notes; and from personal effects recovered from the sea, it was apparent that several of the passengers were agents of different nationalities."*

The plane carried twelve passengers: Three members of 525 Squadron travelling as passengers: RAF Squadron Leader William Godfrey Tiley; RAFVR Flying Officer Noel Spencer Nicklin en route to India; and RAF Pilot Officer George William Lamb.

The nine other passengers included:

George Lionel Seymour Dawson-Damer, Viscount Carlow, Air Commodore, Special Operations Executive (SOE) en route to Yugoslavia;

Ivor Watkins Birts, Lieutenant Colonel, Special Operations Executive (SOE) en route to Yugoslavia;

Stephen Mate (Maitland), Lieutenant, British Army (General List), Special Operations Executive (SOE) en route to Hungary;

Stanley Casson, Lieutenant Colonel, British Intelligence Corps, en route to Greece;

Edmund J Gójski, Captain, Polish Army, Polish Courier en route to Poland;

Józef Król, Major, Polish Forces (Senior Chaplain) en route to Poland;

Thomas Percival Ward, Major, Royal Army Medical Corps;

Roger Achille Albert Baudouin (Boudoin), Commandant, Free French en route to Algiers;

 and Maurice Schwob M.O.S.F.F., Free French Government Agent, travelling from London to Algiers carrying documents to meet with General De Gaulle in Algiers.

The Home Guard Sergeant, the man who had seen the explosion and the aircraft going down into the sea, stated years later: *"The atmosphere in the town was electric. It couldn't have been worse if the Germans had landed. There were a few people around who were thought to be in the know, but if they were they weren't saying anything."*

Every story and every rumour added to the mystery. Just over one week after the crash a Coastguard Officer walking on the beach at Watergate Bay found bits and pieces of wreckage thought to have come from the Warwick, and among them was a corner section of a very well-made box which had the last three letters of a word marked thereon.

The letters were 'ANK', and it was immediately assumed that the full word was BANK and because of the obvious quality of the box, it must have been from the Bank of England.

At this stage talk of gold turned to 'bullion', and because it appeared that the aircraft had only just cleared the cliffs before crashing into the sea, the story got around that it must have gone down like a stone because of the weight of the bullion on board.

Eight days after on April 25, 1944, the body of Flying Officer Gavel was found.

He had sustained serious injuries, was wearing items of clothing of a Canadian Flying Officer Pilot and a wrist watch which had stopped at the time of the crash; however, the identification disc was missing. The body was taken to the mortuary at RAF St Mawgan and identification fell to the "Crash Officer".

He contacted 525 Squadron Adjutant at Lyneham and having established that a personal friend and squadron colleague of Arthur Gavel could identify the wrist watch taken from the body, he arranged for its immediate despatch there by air. There it was seen and positively identified as being that of Arthur Gavel, and this was communicated back to St Mawgan.

All bodies recovered on the morning of April 17, 1944, had injuries consistent with those caused in an air crash; however, Arthur Gavel had other injuries which indicated "proximity to an explosion" and once the Commanding Officer was informed, instructions were issued to prevent viewing or discussion.

On April 26, the body of the pilot was removed from RAF St. Mawgan, the Crash Officer being told it was for specialist post-mortem examination. The personnel assumed that it was because of the injuries caused by an explosion, and which had caused the Station Commander concern.

On April 27, an inquest at Newquay, accepted evidence of a Pathologist, that death was due to drowning and there was no evidence to show how, when, and where the deceased met his death. The body of the pilot was buried with a tombstone inscribed *"Unknown Sailor of the Second World War"* in Fairpark Cemetery, Newquay.

World War II ended in 1945. The parents of the pilot were told the body of their son was never recovered and he would be commemorated on the Runnymede Memorial, England.

The Salvage Vessel failed to find the wreckage in 1944, but local fishermen had trawled their nets for years in Newquay Bay, hoping that one day they will haul up some of the Warwick's 'gold'.

The flight of 525 RAF Squadron Warwick C Mark I, BV247 would become known as the "mystery flight" and the plane itself referred to the "gold plane".

Chief Inspector Derek Fowkes, one of Cornwall's most respected police officers, served in Newquay from 1970 to 1984 and became interested in the crash when he was examining wartime records.

Because of the location where the unidentified body was located, he began to think it could be that of the pilot of the downed Warwick BV247, Flying Officer Arthur Gavel. In 1984, forty years after the crash, Derek Fowkes, in collaboration with Murray W. Gavel of Swift Current, Saskatchewan, the brother of Arthur Gavel, was able to ensure that the body of Arthur Gavel was identified.

Derek Fowkes continued to investigate the unexplained aviation accident, and in 1995 finalized an extensive report on his discoveries. He interviewed surviving primary and secondary witness; checked all documentary evidence compiled at the time by those in authority; considered circumstantial evidence and corroborated hearsay evidence; and finally drew inferences from a series of unexplained coincidences.

A Court of Enquiry was convened within 48 hours of the loss of the aircraft and its report was confusing.

Derek Fowkes assumed it was intentionally in order to cloud the issues involved. Double British Summer Time (OBST) was in force in England at that time, and while most people were using it, operations personnel on the airfield, including the Flying Control Officers, were using GMT, and throughout the report there is an obvious two-hour difference in what some people are talking about.

For example, the Warwick departed at 0040 GMT (0240 OBST) with no problem with starting, taxiing out, and take-off, but a Mailcan Fortress which departed at 0240 GMT had flame out on one engine at starting, and was backfiring on one engine during take-off.

When the Warwick took off there was no other aircraft in circuit, but when the Fortress took off there was. When the Warwick took off there was no mist on the edge of the airfield, but when the Fortress took off there was.

The President of the Court of Inquiry, who presumably was responsible for submitting the report, knew of this confusion, and yet he chose to base his findings on evidence which clearly related to the Fortress. The Report speculates on fog as a factor but failed to call the duty Met Officer or the Briefing Officer, both of whom could have confirmed there was not any when the Warwick departed. There was a procession of aircraft taking off that night - both before and after BV247, and there was no problem with fog.

The Court speculated on the possibility of an engine failure on a heavily laden aircraft on take-off and ignored the evidence of the airfield controller who said that lift-off and climb-out was perfectly normal.

They speculated on the presence of another aircraft supposedly in circuit prior to landing at an adjacent airfield. but there was no second aircraft at the time the Warwick took off, and flight schedules for St Mawgan and the adjoining St Eval clearly show that the only time there were two aircraft in circuit at the same time was two hours after the Warwick had gone.

One disturbing aspect of the Court of Inquiry Report is the withholding of the evidence of the one eyewitness, the Home Guard Sergeant.

He was interviewed by crash investigators and his statement taken, but he was not called to give evidence. Surprisingly, his Commanding Officer was called to 'present' the sergeant's evidence, but there is no copy of the Sergeant's statement, or reference to the Lieutenant or the Sergeant in the report.

In his statement the Sergeant described the effect of the explosion, its colours, and then what was obviously an aircraft falling away with sparks and flame trails behind. He held the position of the explosion with his arm outraised till soldiers with him placed a five-foot length of antenna against crossed bayonets in the ground to hold the line and angle. He did a flash to bang count which gave an approximate distance measure, and he described the bang, when it came as a sort of woolly - bursting paper-bag sound.

The Sergeant was an experienced radio engineer/operator engaged in training regular soldiers in the use of radio equipment, and immediately reported what he had seen and heard on an Air/Sea Rescue frequency to an Air Sea Rescue Unit at RAF St Eval.

The fact that the Home Guard Sergeant's report of an explosion was received, understood, and acted on, is confirmed, by coded signals sent in the early hours of April 17, 1944, by OAC (Overseas Air Control) 44 Group Gloucester.

The first signal in REKOH SYKO (code) was to DNY-A, asking - *"Are you in trouble"*, and when there was no response, the second was sent to Gibraltar, and after giving details of the departure of DNY-A said *"Explosion reported from direction of sea shortly after take-off. Signal urgent if, repeat if, this aircraft arrives"*.

Two other records are at variance with the finding of the Court of Inquiry.525 Squadron O.R.B., and 44 Group Transport Command accident report for April 1944, both refer to the loss of BV247, and both state this was due to an "explosion" shortly after take-off.

While the Court of Inquiry was in session, there were two happenings, both of which should, one would have thought, at least in the mind of Derek Fowkes, have been referred to the Court, but which were not. First a Salvage Vessel arrived in Newquay Bay with terms of reference: "find the wreckage of BV247 at all costs" and the second, the body of the missing Warwick Pilot Arthur Gavel was recovered.

With regard to the Salvage Vessel Joy Bell III on charter to the Air Ministry, enquiries by Derek Fowkes indicated that this was an operation organized by the American OSS (Office of Strategic Services; a wartime intelligence agency of the United States during World War II) and two of their officers were on board throughout a four-day search. They were hoping to recover a diplomatic bag which one of two French passengers had been carrying to General de Gaulle in Algiers.

At the same time, an RAF Salvage Officer (RAF St Mawgan) was interested in recovering a valuable British cargo, but the operation failed because they couldn't locate the wreckage.

Fowkes's investigation into the recovery and disposal of the body of Arthur Douglas Gavel raised a number of questions.

The body of Flying Officer Arthur Douglas Gavel was found on the beach at Whipsiderry Beach, Newquay Bay on April 25, 1944, just eight days after the crash.

The body had sustained serious injuries, was clothed in a RCAF uniform, and wore a wrist watch which had stopped at the time of the crash.

The WWII routine for bodies recovered from the sea was for them to be taken to a Newquay Urban District Council mortuary, but if the body were obviously that of an airman, it would be taken to the mortuary at RAF St Mawgan, and that is what happened to the body found on April 25, 1944, on Whipsiderry Beach. It was obviously the body of an airman.

The Crash Officer had forwarded the wrist watch for identification and whilst awaiting the reply, he ascertained that the FCO (Flying Control Officer) at St Mawgan had spoken with the Pilot of the Warwick during his stop-over at St Mawgan, and so it was arranged for him to view the body.

The Flying Control Officer was contacted by the Station Medical Office who said: - "*We think we have the body of the big Canadian Pilot from the Warwick*". The Flying Control Officer visited the mortuary and confirmed that in his opinion it was the body of the pilot.

Because of the very brief contact, and the fact that the identification disc was missing, he was happy to think that his identification was to be confirmed by the watch, and that was the end of his involvement.

The Medical Officer concerned by the condition of the pilot's body had "put a clamp" on the mortuary and issued instructions to prevent viewing or discussion.

The routine which should have been followed at that point in time is clearly set out in Home Office Circular No.987 of 13th August 1942.

This says: "*any male member of any air force who dies from injuries sustained by him in the course of his duties which are ascribable to an accident in which an aircraft belonging to an air force is involved, shall be deemed for the purposes of paras 3 to 6(A) of the Defence (Burials, Inquests and Registration of Deaths) Regulations 1942 to have died in the consequence of "war operations"*.

The circular continues: "*In these cases, therefore, no person is required to inform the coroner of the death and a coroner shall not be obliged or authorised to take any action in relation to the death unless the Secretary of State otherwise directs*".

Fowkes concluded this routine was clearly understood by the Station Commander, and in fact he had complied with the regulations on April 17 when fourteen other bodies from the Warwick had been taken to his station. There was no post-mortem and no inquest on any of those bodies. He merely forwarded a list of names to the Registrar of Deaths at Newquay, certifying death as due to "war operations" and thereafter made arrangements for proper service-burials.

With regard to burial, Fowkes understood that it was normal to consult next of kin, in cases where this was possible, or in the case of Commonwealth and Foreign nationals, their governments, and some of the crew and passengers from BV247 are buried at Newquay, some at Brookwood Military Cemetery, and others in their home-cemeteries. One body was taken to London and lodged in a catacomb to await transfer home, overseas, after the war.

Fowkes could not think of any reason why this routine wasn't applied to the pilot, Arthur Gavel. Instead on the April 26 "someone" arranged for the body to be taken away, with the Staff Medical Officer and the Crash Officer being told it was for specialist post-mortem examination. Fowkes concluded they assumed that it was because of the injuries caused by an explosion, and which had caused the Station Commander such concern.

What happened to the body when it left RAF St Mawgan is not known, but on the April 27, just one day later and then described as being that of an 'unknown male", it was subject of an inquest at Newquay.

The evidence of a Pathologist was accepted by the HM Coroner and the death was recorded as due to drowning. He then added a rider; "*there being no evidence to show how, when and where the deceased met his death*".

Derek Fowkes was told that all HM Coroners records for this period had been destroyed, and Fowkes was unable to establish the identity of the pathologist who certified the cause of death of an 'unknown male' as being due to drowning.

In WWII there was only one person engaged in that line of work in the County of Cornwall. He had no deputy.

He was responsible for all post-mortem examinations, civilian and service. Those involving airmen from St Mawgan were carried out on the Station.

According to Fowkes, the pathologist knew all about the crash of BV247 and said, *"everyone did, but denied all knowledge of Pilot Arthur Gavel and the unknown male, and claimed to have no records for that period".*

Derek Fowkes believed the circumstances of the disposal of the body of Arthur Gavel, have the hallmark of a conspiracy, and there are questions that remain unanswered:

Who authorised the removal of the body of a Canadian Air Force Officer from the mortuary at RAF St Mawgan?

Who notified the Local authority that it was that of an unknown male?

Who was the pathologist who wrongly recorded the cause of death as drowning?

Who informed HM Coroner that - *"there was no evidence to show how, when or where the deceased had met his death"?*

Who gave the Commonwealth War Graves Commission information which resulted in them erecting a tombstone over Arthur Gavel's grave inscribed *"Unknown Sailor of the Second World War"?*

It has been suggested to Fowkes that all this could have been due to wartime sloppiness, but if so, who by? The Station Commander, the Station Adjutant who knew about the identification of the watch, the Pathologist, His Majesty's Coroner, the Officers of the Local Authority?

Fowkes believed there were too many people involved for that to be the case. he believed the problem lay with the pilot's injuries.

An explosion had occurred on board Warwick BV 247, but a 'decision' had been made to conceal that fact and all evidence of it had been excluded from the Court of Inquiry report. Fowkes concluded there had to be influence exerted from a pretty high level to organise that sort of thing, and it obviously had.

Then just as the President of the Court of Inquiry was submitting his 'cover-up' report, in came the body of Arthur Gavel with explosive-injuries to the trunk, and consternation reigned again. The Station Commander put an immediate embargo on the mortuary, ordered the Station Medical Officer to say nothing of the injuries to anyone and within twenty-four hours the body had gone. That had to be a pretty quick move by any standards.

Fowkes could only conclude that the body was disposed of in furtherance of a conspiracy to conceal that an explosion had taken place on board BV247.

Whatever the reason, the cruellest act came when Arthur Gavel's parents back in Swift Current, Saskatchewan, Canada, were notified, that he was missing, with a date of death presumed to be April 17, 1944.   His loss, and the realisation that there was no known grave where the family could pay their respects was a final blow. Sadly, the Gavel family - thousands of miles away in Canada, were not able to question what had happened, but this changed in 1980 as a result of what can only be described as *'an intervention of fate'*.

Arising from RAF reunions of those who had served at RAF St Mawgan in 1944, and those who had flown with 525 Squadron, it was learned that Arthur Gavel's body had in fact been recovered and identified in April 1944.

An investigation to find out what had happened to it quickly focussed attention on a grave at Fairpark Cemetery, Newquay, which was marked as being that of an 'Unknown Seaman'.

The attitude of the 'authorities' to a request for information, and for exhumation for identification purposes was for Fowkes, unhelpful to say the least, but in 1984, forty years after the crash, exhumation went ahead and was positive.

The authorities paid for a proper re-burial service, and the placement of a correctly inscribed tombstone, but no-one offered any apology to the family or explanation for what happened. It was just left for them to accept that it was one of the sort of things that happened in war.

But, according to the investigation by Derek Fowkes, it was not quite like that. There had been an explosion, and if it was a 'normal 'act of war', there was no requirement for the Court of Inquiry to organise a cover up - but it had.

Fowkes learned that several top secret signals, using RAF Form 683 Secret Cipher, were sent on the night of April 16/17, 1944, to Air Ministry, Transport Command and Group HQ reporting that an explosion had been seen and reported shortly after the Warwick had taken off and when it was over the sea.

There was concern later that day when the Station Commander issued an instruction that there must be no further reference to 'explosion' in any station records or in any further signals and this led to a belief that some sort of 'Sikorski' operation was involved "to get rid of someone".

Fowkes learned that the situation was reviewed, following the event and there was a knowledge that an explosion had occurred at about 2000 feet when the Warwick was out over the sea and that all evidence of it was to be excluded from the report of the Court of Inquiry and the Court's report was a cover-up. The crash had been written off as due to possible fog or engine failure, but this was not true - it was due to sabotage and not by the enemy.

Because of a concern such an event could happen again, the passenger list was reviewed to see if it included the sort of person some secret organisation might want to get rid of, and the result was a focus on Roger Achille Albert Baudouin (Boudoin), Commandant, Free French and Maurice Schwob M.O.S.F.F., Free French Government Agent, travelling from London to Algiers - simply because the Americans had been seeking to recover the French diplomatic bag from the wreckage and at that time just six weeks before D-Day, everyone was paranoid about security and de Gaulle's Free French were considered a risk.

A lot of time was spent trying to work out what sort of device could have been used; how it could have been taken on board; where it had been placed; and how it was triggered. But, timing and mechanical devices were out because of the twenty-four hour delay, and it became impossible to determine how an explosive device would be used.

Fowkes considered the unusual aspect of the crash. It was subject of an investigation by the American Counter Intelligence Corp.

Under normal circumstances the Warwick would have been no concern, but RAF St Mawgan was a joint RAF/USATC base, and the Americans were told it was suspected that an explosive device had been placed on board the Warwick, and that it had detonated just after take-off when the plane was out over the sea.

Their investigation, Fowkes learned, was not so much aimed at establishing the cause, as covering their backs. While the British and Americans were Allies in the war and generally got along quite well, each service tended to protect its own and did not ask or get any help from the other in time of trouble.

The American investigator was given clearance for enquiries round the base but was asked to oblige with a report which just negatived any suggestion of American involvement and asked it "kindly" not refer to rumours and explosion.

The "Crash of British Warwick Aircraft", together with a confidential covering report which gave slightly more detail was submitted and as a matter of routine ended in the US Army Intelligence and Security Command Archives at Fort Meade, Maryland. Unfortunately, a fire in 1973 destroyed more than 75% of the records, including the 'Warwick' report.

The open report negated any American involvement. But, once again the Sikorski crash at Gibraltar was still very much in everyone's mind, and this prompted the belief by the American investigator at the time that the British Secret Service or some such organisation had been involved with the intention of getting rid of someone.

In one interview during his investigation, Fowkes was told: *"Let me cast grave doubts on sabotage. First, why? None of the people on board looks like a target for such an act. Secondly the technical problem of causing a devastating explosion undetected at that time, almost insuperable".*

Fowkes accepted that for sabotage, there would have to be a target. If the objective were to get rid of someone on an aircraft in flight over the sea there would have to be a device capable of achieving that objective and there would have to be a means of placing it on board without being detected or arousing suspicion, and finally there had to be an "organisation" involved in that line of business.

However, from the research by Fowkes, he learned of a likely target among the passengers and knowledge that a barometric device for getting rid of an aircraft in flight, and the means of infiltrating it on board an aircraft did exist in 1944.

The barometrically detonated explosive device, specially manufactured to destroy an aircraft in flight could have been placed on board a guarded aircraft such as the Warwick in a diplomatic bag.

Two diplomatic bags had been put on board the Warwick just prior to take-off. If those bags were genuine their loss would be recorded in a Foreign Office Index in the Public Record Office at Kew. If they were not genuine, there will be no record.

Fowkes checked he index, found the section which recorded the losses of diplomatic, departmental, and secret mail bags, but there is no record of the loss of SM 18 and SM 19.

The two bags on the night of April 16/17, 1944, were addressed to an office at Maison Blanche known by the letters I.S.L.D (Inter Services Liaison Department). The bags were of normal brief-case size, of canvas, and with specially weighted bottoms, said to ensure they would not float off into enemy hands in the event of the aircraft crashing into the sea.

The despatch of such items was routinely signalled all the way along the line, and their despatch was signalled to 44 Group HQ Gloucester in a signal timed 170040 (0040hrs April 17, 1944), but after the crash the details of the two bags were queried by Group HQ.

It was then found that the information on file at St Mawgan was insufficient to identify the office of origin and rules and regulations were tightened up to cover the future receipt and despatch, but the question as to where those bags had come from and what they had contained was never resolved.

The only record that the two bags existed is to be found in the Court of Inquiry report and this refers to the handing over to the pilot of secret bags marked SM18 and SM19. No issue was made about the bags at the Inquiry, but the evidence clearly indicates that two 'mysterious' bags went on board minutes before take-off. One or other could have contained an explosive device.

There is one other reference to the barometric-device and that is in a book "Clandestine Warfare" published 1988,

"The inventors had in mind its use behind or under a pilot's seat in a plane carrying VIPs who after the explosion would be killed when the plane crashed".

The Investigation by Derek Fowkes concluded:

Most of Art Gavel's friends in 525 Squadron assumed that he had suffered an engine failure during climb out, and that with a heavy load, passengers, freight, and fuel, he went straight down into the sea, but it did not happen like that.

The possibility of an "engine blow-out" was also discussed within the Squadron. A 525 Pilot had a nasty experience during take-off when this occurred, leaving bits and pieces of the engine and a load of oil all over the runway, but the Engineering Officer put that down to 'hydraulicing'.

Hydraulicing arises when those responsible for servicing a radial engine aircraft, fail to drain off accumulated oil in the bottom cylinders in between flights.

As soon as pressure is applied at run-up, or at the commencement of take-off, the bottoms are blown out of one or more of the bottom cylinders, but this did not happen to BV247.

The question of the Pilot being caught out by the 'up-draught' which occurred at the cliff-edge when taking off out over the sea was discussed, but this was a problem which appertained at RAF Station Portreath further down the coast where the runway went right up to the top of the cliff. There was not the same problem at St Mawgan where the end of the runway was away from the cliff.

An explosion was seen, heard, reported, and acted on, and that "explosion" is recorded as the cause of the crash in 525 Squadron ORB and in 44 Group crash-records.

The Court of Inquiry excluded evidence which clearly indicated that an explosion had occurred on board BV247, and that the Court's report was a cover-up, and there had to be a reason for it.

The body of Art Gavel was recovered and identified and disposed of, and there had to be a reason for it. The "authorities" were unhappy about Fowkes' "historic investigation". He was asked *"why are you poking your nose into this?"* and *"do everyone a favour and leave it alone"*.

When he asked to see a copy of The Court of Inquiry report, he was told that those sorts of reports had long since been destroyed. The report had not been destroyed.

With regard to the exhumation of what he believed to be Arthur Gavel's remains, he was told he would never get a Home Office Licence for exhumation for identification purposes; and when he applied for Arthur Gavel's medical and dental records for identification purposes, he was told the next of kin was not entitled to them, nor was he, their personal representative.

Senior officers on the station, and the Americans were talking of sabotage, not by the enemy, but by the British Secret Service or some similar organisation.

There were some fascinating people on board the Warwick. One of two French passengers M. Maurice Schwob was carrying a secret file intending to present it to General De Gaulle in Algiers and publish it. It contained information authorities would not want made public.

The second French passenger - Commandant Roger Achille Albert Baudouin, a cryptanalyst, had worked at the Top-Secret Government Communications HQ at Bletchley Park and had knowledge which could prejudice the security of D-Day. The British and American security services did not trust General de Gaulle and his 'Committee'.

From midnight of the day of the crash April 17, 1944, a complete travel ban came into force to protect the security of D-Day, and under the circumstances it is hard to understand why the Foreign Office had granted an Air Passage Authority for such a man to travel on what was to be 'the last plane to Algiers'.

A Mark II barometric device had been manufactured specifically to destroy an aircraft in flight.

The two mysterious Secret Mail Bags were taken on board the Warwick just prior to take-off, and they could have provided the means whereby an explosive device was inveigled on board and into a position behind the Pilot's seat.

Derek Fowkes concluded the loss of the aircraft was due to sabotage and covered up - and not by the enemy.

The Warwick flight, however, remains a 'classic deniable accident' by official agencies, and with no clear evidence, it is officially "deniable".

Sources:

"An Investigation into the Cause of the Crash of British Warwick C. MK. I Aircraft BV247 of 525 Squadron, RAF Transport Command" Derek Fowkes (December 1995)

http://www.wartimeheritage.com/storyarchive2/storymysteryflight.htm

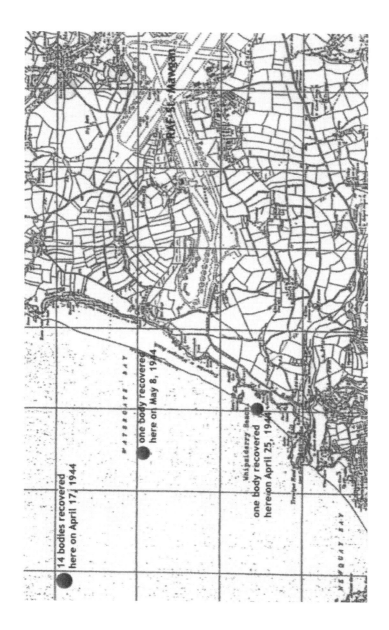

A view of the military graves at of Fairpark Cemetery, Newquay
(Source: www.cwgc.com)

STANLEY CASSON'S FINAL RESTING PLACE
Fairpark Cemetery, Rialton Road, St. Columb Minor, TR7 3EA

Stanley Casson is one of 33 WW2 casualties who are buried in the council operated Fairview Cemetery near Newquay in Cornwall.

The cemetery is located on the edge of the picturesque village of St Columb Minor - which is on the A3059 road that leads into Newquay when approaching from the A39 and A392.

The Commonwealth War Graves Commission website explains that:

Newquay (Fairpark) Cemetery contains 33 Second World War burials. Of these, 20 are together in a group of 23, the remaining three being the graves of ex-servicemen who were buried in the war graves group, although their deaths were not due to war service. Seven unidentified men of the Merchant Navy are also buried in this cemetery.

Stanley occupies grave 684 of the Church of England plot - and next to him in grave 685 is Lt-Col Ivor Birts of the SOE, who was killed in the same air crash.

Of the other casualties from the crash, Lt. Steven Maitland is buried in grave 686 under his original name of Steven Mate, Flying Officer Arthur Douglas Gavel is in grave 687 and Flight Sergeant Michael Kingston Rowe is in grave 705.

The cemetery is not far from RAF St Mawgan which is the base that Stanley's fatal flight took off from and, according to the RAF website www.raf.mod.uk, is used today as a:

No 22 (Training) Group Station that provides a platform for future and current operations in the south west. The Station is home to the Defence Survive, Evade, Resist, Extract (SERE) Training Organisation (known as DSTO), and supports the Remote Radar Head at Portreath – part of the air defence system for the UK.

LIEUTENANT COLONEL
S CASSON

INTELLIGENCE CORPS
17th APRIL 1944 AGE 54

MANY SHALL COMMEND HIS
UNDERSTANDING; AND WHILE
THE WORLD ENDURETH IT
SHALL NOT BE BLOTTED OUT

Photo of Casson's headstone (Source www.findagrave.com / Photo by Sheila W)

Stanley Casson on WorldCat

The WorldCat database is a fascinating tool for researchers as it lists practically every book that is held in a library anywhere.

It is run by OCLC, which is a global library cooperative that provides shared technology services, original research and community programs for its membership and the library community at large.

You can find out more about them at these websites:
https://www.oclc.org/en/worldcat.html
https://www.worldcat.org/

The entry on WorldCat for Stanley Casson lists 165 works in 653 publications in 5 languages and 7,084 library holdings.

Most widely held works about Stanley Casson:

- filéllên Stanley Casson by Hrist Haralámpous

- Bibliography: Lieut.-Colonel Stanley Casson, (Intelligence Corps.) M.A., F.S.A., Hon. A.R.I.B.A

Most widely held works by Stanley Casson in WorldCat Libraries:

The Technique Of Early Greek Sculpture by Stanley Casson
40 editions published between 1923 and 2013 in 3 languages

Some Modern Sculptors by Stanley Casson
23 editions published between 1928 and 1967 in English

XXth Century Sculptors by Stanley Casson
17 editions published between 1930 and 1967 in English

Macedonia, Thrace and Illyria; their relations to Greece from the earliest times down to the time of Philip son of Amyntas by Stanley Casson
42 editions published between 1925 and 1971 in 3 languages

Ancient Cyprus; its art and archaeology by Stanley Casson
31 editions published between 1937 and 2018 in English

Progress of Archaeology by Stanley Casson
24 editions published between 1934 and 1935 in English

The Discovery of Man; The story of the inquiry into human origins by Stanley Casson
26 editions published between 1939 and 1941 in English

A Brief History Of The Twin Studies Of Archaeology & Anthropology - Greece Against The Axis by Stanley Casson
21 editions published between 1941 and 1943 in English

Progress And Catastrophe; An Anatomy Of Human Adventure by Stanley Casson
16 editions published in 1937 in English

Greece and Britain by Stanley Casson
24 editions published between 1943 and 1965 in English and Greek, Modern

Sculpture of to-day by Stanley Casson
13 editions published in 1939 in English

Greece and the Ægean by Ernest Arthur Gardner
16 editions published between 1933 and 1938 in English

Ancient Greece by Stanley Casson
12 editions published in 1922 in English

Greece by Stanley Casson
19 editions published between 1941 and 1943 in 3 languages

Catalogue of the Acropolis Museum by Mouseio Akropolēs
4 editions published in 1921 in English

Rupert Brooke and Skyros by Stanley Casson
3 editions published in 1921 in English

Ancient Greece by Stanley Casson
11 editions published in 1939 in English

Chypre dans l'Antiquité by Stanley Casson
12 editions published in 1939 in French

Hellenic studies by Stanley Casson
7 editions published in 1920 in English

You can read and download many of Stanley Casson's books completely free of charge at

www.archive.org

UNE MARCHE POUR COMMÉMORER ET SE RESSOURCER

THE WESTERN FRONT WAY

Sauvegarder le passé en éduquant les générations futures

The Western Front Way – by Lucy London

The Western Front Way is a new, continuous, permanent, marked path from the Swiss border in the South through France and Belgium to the channel coast in the North.

The path for peace is a memorial conceived by Rory Forsyth and inspired by a letter home from the Front during the First World War, sent in 1915 by Alexander Douglas Gillespie, who saw a time after the conflict and a way of healing the ravages of war. He wrote:

"... when peace comes, our government might combine with the French government to make one long avenue between the lines from the Vosges to the sea...a fine broad road in the 'No Mans Land' between the lines, with paths for pilgrims".

Interestingly enough, Stanley Casson also contemplated the idea of such a pathway back in his 1935 book "Steady Drummer", when he wrote:

"Night in the trenches was the most enduring experience of all. I used to wonder how long it would take me to walk from the beaches of the North Sea to that curious end of all fighting against the Swiss boundary."

The Logo adopted by The Western Front Way depicts the four flowers of remembrance:

The Cornflower (bluet), which is the remembrance flower of France, the Daisy (madeliefje) of Belgium, the Forget-me-Not (Vergiss-mein nicht) of Germany & The Red Flanders Poppy

The use of the poppy is universal but the original idea of using it as a symbol of remembrance comes from American Poet Moina Belle Michael's vow always to wear a red poppy in remembrance.

The Western Front Way have just announced that you can purchase a marker with the 4 flowers of commemoration for France, Germany, Belgium & The Commonwealth for £5 and be a legacy for collaboration and peace.

Visit their website & find out how to order your waymarkers: https://www.thewesternfrontway.com/

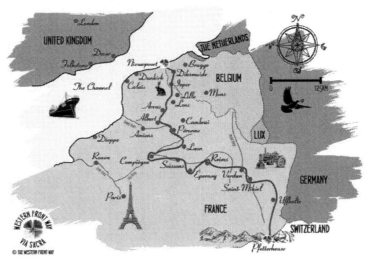

Made in the USA
Columbia, SC
01 September 2022

65854728R00074